Jeff Allen's Best:
Win the Job

Other books by Jeffrey G. Allen, J.D., C.P.C.

HOW TO TURN AN INTERVIEW INTO A JOB
(also available on audiocassette)

FINDING THE RIGHT JOB AT MIDLIFE

THE PLACEMENT STRATEGY HANDBOOK

THE EMPLOYEE TERMINATION HANDBOOK

PLACEMENT MANAGEMENT

SURVIVING CORPORATE DOWNSIZING

THE COMPLETE Q&A JOB INTERVIEW BOOK

THE PERFECT JOB REFERENCE

JEFF ALLEN'S BEST: THE RESUME

JEFF ALLEN'S BEST: GET THE INTERVIEW

Jeff Allen's Best: Win the Job

Jeffrey G. Allen, J.D., C.P.C.

John Wiley & Sons, Inc.

New York • Chichester • Brisbane • Toronto • Singapore

Library of Congress Cataloging-in-Publication Data

Allen, Jeffrey G., 1943—
    Jeff Allen's best: win the job / Jeffrey G. Allen.
        p. cm.
    Includes bibliographical references.
    ISBN 0471-52550-2 (c). ISBN 0471-525551-0 (pbk)
    1. Employment interviewing.   I. Title.
HF5549.5.I6A443   1990   90-36153
650.14—dc20   CIP

Printed in the United States of America

91   10 9 8 7 6 5 4 3 2

Printed and bound by the Courier Companies, Inc.

To the countless number of personnel consultants and jobseekers whose successes fill the pages of this series. May your "best" instruct and inspire countless others to succeed.

With appreciation . . .

To my wife, Bev;
to our daughter, Angela;
to an editor's editor, Mike Hamilton,
    who conceived the series;
and to Louann Werksma,
    who assisted with its research and development.

You definitely keep me at

"Jeff Allen's best!"

About the Author

Jeffrey G. Allen, J.D., C.P.C., is America's leading placement attorney and Director of the National Placement Law Center in Los Angeles. Experience as a certified placement counselor, personnel manager, and professional negotiator uniquely qualifies him to write this breakthrough three-part series on techniques that will result in getting and winning the maximum number of job interviews.

Mr. Allen is the author of more bestselling books in the career field than anyone else. Among them are *How to Turn an Interview into a Job*, *Finding the Right Job at Midlife*, *The Placement Strategy Handbook*, *Placement Management*, *The Complete Q&A Job Interview Book*, and *The Perfect Job Reference*. He writes a nationally syndicated column entitled "Placements and the Law," conducts seminars, and is regularly featured in television, radio, and newspaper interviews.

Mr. Allen has been appointed Special Advisor to the American Employment Association, is General Counsel to the California Association of Personnel Consultants, and is nationally recognized as the foremost authority in the specialty of placement law.

Contents

Introduction   **1**

1   Rehearsal: Prepare for Your Performance   **7**

   1. Schedule for success.   9
   2. Limit interviews to 45 minutes.   10
   3. Avoid meal interviews.   10
   4. Eliminate fear of the unknown.   11
   5. Complete an application in advance.   14
   6. Deputize internal referrals.   14
   7. Dress the part and the part plays itself.   14
   8. The interviewing uniform for men.   15
   9. The interviewing uniform for women.   16
 10. Carry an attache case.   17
 11. Know the exceptions to the wardrobe rule.   18
 12. Fuel your jobgetting engine.   18
 13. Arrive alone.   19
 14. Arrive on time.   20
 15. Don't arrive early, either.   20
 16. Review your notes.   21
 17. Acclimate to your environment.   21
 18. Don't wait more than a half hour for the interviewer.   22
 19. Don't wear a coat, hat, or other outdoor clothing into the interview.   22
 20. Don't wear sunglasses.   22
 21. Have your script well rehearsed.   23

2   The Script: Know the Answers in Advance   **25**

 22. Use the "programmed interview system" to fast-forward your future.   27

23. Scan the script.   29
24. Customize it to the target job.   29
25. Customize it to your "character."   29
26. Record and replay.   29
27. Rehearse your delivery.   29
28. Repeat it 'till it rolls off your tongue.   30
29. Personal questions: Know the knockout factors.   30
30. Educational background questions: Show what you know.   34
31. Character questions: Be careful!   40
32. Initiative and creativity questions: Focus on what and why.   45
33. Questions about management ability: You're an "MBA."   50
34. Career objective questions: Make it clear what they hear.   56
35. Questions about the target job: You suit it to a "t"!   60
36. Questions about salary history and requirements: Get more!   68
37. Experience and training questions: You've got the experience
    express card!   72
38. "Outside interest" questions can get you *inside*!   76
39. Your turn: Questions to ask the interviewer.   80

3   The Screen Test: Your Interview   83

40. Make the first impression the best.   85
41. Use the "magic four hello."   86
42. Hone your handshake.   86
43. Don't address the interviewer by his or her first name.   87
44. Avoid assuming a subordinate role.   87
45. Admire something in the interviewer's office.   88
46. Assess the interviewer's style.   88
47. Recognize the four basic personality types.   88
48. Align with the interviewer   92
49. Attempt to sit next to the interviewer.   94
50. "Mirror" the interviewer's body language, facial expressions,
    eye movement, rate of speech, tone of voice, and rate of
    breathing.   94
51. Use "insider" language.   95
52. Develop an action vocabulary.   98
53. Write the winner's word list into your script.   99
54. Choose and use success phrases.   100
55. Don't use trite phrases and tired cliches.   101
56. Withhold your resume.   102

57. Use the "tie-down" technique to move the interview along.   102
58. The standard tie-down.   103
59. The inverted tie-down.   104
60. The internal tie-down.   104
61. The tag-on tie-down.   104
62. Find an area of agreement, and lead slowly and carefully
    to the offer.   105
63. Be honest, not modest.   106
64. Say positive things about your present (or former) employer. 106
65. Admire the achievements of the prospective employer.   107
66. Be observant.   107
67. Package a positive image.   108

INTERVIEW "DON'TS"

68. Don't smoke.   109
69. Don't chew gum.   109
70. Don't interrupt.   110
71. Don't object to discriminatory questions.   110
72. Don't look at your watch.   110
73. Don't read any documents on the interviewer's desk.   110
74. Don't pick up any objects in the interviewer's office.   111
75. Don't ask for the job.   111
76. Use the "magic four good-bye."   111

4 Getting the Part: Follow-up and Finishing Touches   113

77. Image the interview.   115
78. Recap your revelations.   116
79. Write your review.   116
80. Write a follow-up letter.   116
81. Follow the better letter format.   118
82. Create the content carefully.   119
83. Don't fiddle around.   120
84. Take a deep breath—and call the interviewer.   121
85. Call your references.   122
86. Recontact your internal referrals.   123
87. Prepare for your encore performance.   123
88. The "Who Are You?" interview.   125
89. The "What Can You Do for Us?" interview   125
90. Negotiate the terms of employment.   125

 91. Clarify the job description.   126
 92. Secure a star's salary.   126
 93. Get an offer in writing.   127
 94. Evaluate the offer.   127
 95. Accept with assurance.   127
 96. Resign with refinement.   128
 97. Leave 'em laughing.   128
 98. Get a reference letter.   128
 99. Thank your supporting cast.   128
100. Begin again.   129

Conclusion   **131**

Endnotes   **135**

Bibliography   **137**

Index   **139**

Jeff Allen's Best:
Win the Job

Introduction

Almost 25 years have passed since I began helping people get hired.

I can still feel the thrill of my second placement. My *first* was getting myself hired—as a corporate recruiter. But getting someone *else* hired convinced me a job interview is nothing more than a screen test. An act.

The hiring process will never change. It depends almost completely on the "actor factor." If you get the "casting director's" attention, know your lines, perfect your delivery, and dress for the part, you'll get hired. If you don't, you won't. One big break. No retake.

After my starting role as a corporate recruiter, I spent almost a decade behind a personnel "director's" desk, conducting countless casting calls in hundreds of hiring halls. Interviewing hopeful hirees of every age, stage, and wage, every day (and night—in my sleep). I followed their trials and errors, successes and failures, hits and bombs.

I never viewed that second placement as "beginner's luck." No self-respecting recruiter would. They tell you a lot of reasons why they're successful, but luck isn't among them. After using the techniques in *Jeff Allen's Best*, you'll agree. There's a systematic, consistent, predictable way for anyone to get hired—almost anywhere.

If you look through other "career" books on the shelf, you'll see how "secret" the formula still is. Each author suggests a different approach. Look long enough, and you'll find that half contradict the other half. Some are philosophical, others motivational, and still others personal. Judging by the number of books available on the topic, you'd think everyone who ever got a job is an "expert" on how to get one.

In 1983, Simon & Schuster approached me to write *How to Turn an Interview into a Job*. Its vice-president and senior editor had received a command from the president: "Get that guy!" Nobody knew how the techniques were developed, but they heard how powerfully they worked. I remember the VP's exact words: "We sure can help a lot of people with this book." He was right. We sure did. Probably millions by now. Their success stories are playing on corporate "stages" around the world. They're starring in the roles they do so well. Receiving rave reviews. Writing their own tickets.

Now I specialize in placement law. Thousands of recruiters call and write the National Placement Law Center every year to discuss their placements. Thousands of jobseekers call to report on their successes. "Seconds" become superstars, their careers straight up, their futures assured. Our work continues, as we constantly refine the openers, deliveries, and scripts. But the audience preferences never change. The reaction is always the same: rave reviews. Only more predictably and consistently.

Getting and winning interviews is easy and fun once you know the way. Only the theaters and audiences change—the places and faces—never the reactions. You only need to learn the techniques once, and you're set for life.

I know. You think "background," "qualifications," or "experience" have something to do with getting hired. You're right—not about the *job*, though. About *getting* the job! The director only knows what you show. That's why the actor factor is so "critical."

Through the years, I developed the only measure of jobgetting that counts: the *interview-to-offer ratio*. If you ask enough people, you'll find it averages twelve to one. It takes *twelve* interviews for the average person to get *one* job offer. That means for every person who intuitively knows how to get hired every time (or uses the techniques in this series), some walking wounded is limping into his or her *twenty-fourth* interview. For every two people who get the part on their first screen test, there's someone being carried into his or her *forty-eighth*! Destroyed, not employed.

"Almost chosen" doesn't count. Either you're in or you're out. When you're hot, you're hot. And when you're *not*—"Don't call us, we'll call you."

After a while, these folks live with a self-fulfilling prophecy: rejection. They might as well just call the interviewer and say, "I'm canceling the interview. Your time is too valuable to waste with me." They're destined to flub their lines from the time the first board claps.

Tragic. Even more tragic when that interview-to-offer ratio will tumble down for *anyone* who'll just use the three books that comprise *Jeff Allen's Best*. The techniques I share for writing your resume, getting an interview, and winning the interview aren't philosophical, motivational, or personal. They're the ones that work every time the curtain goes up. Start ad-libbing, and you'll spend your career making a career out of making a career. If something works, it's in this three-part miniseries. If it doesn't, it's not.

I've long since proven that the best person for the job is someone who can get hired. That's because the people who get the leading roles are the people who are promoted faster, have more self-esteem, and bounce back from the ravages of corporate life faster and higher than anyone else.

So, let's get busy. No more "extra" status. No more understudy roles. No more "bit parts," either. Nuthin' to hit but the heights. Your name in lights. I'll be your coach, manager, and even your agent for a while. Come with me into the winners' world of work. Through the back entrance, in the elevator, up to the office with the star on the door.

The techniques in the three books in this series will get you interviewed and lower the interview-to-offer ratio to around *three* to one. Not because I want them to, not because you need them to, but because they're based on a quarter-century of trial and error. The same way every breakthrough since the dawn of civilization has occurred. Soon you'll see that exploring your career world and discovering yourself in the process is more enlightening, more exciting, and even more enjoyable than all the silver screen scenarios you'll ever watch.

You need training in three specific areas to get hired in a target job—writing your resume, getting interviews, and interviewing to obtain job offers. In this volume, we'll discuss winning the job.

Chapter

1

Rehearsal: Prepare for Your Performance

After 25 years in the job placement field, I've learned three basic truths:

1. The interview is a screen test—an act.
2. The interview is almost all that counts.
3. The interview is a rehearsable, predictable, controllable event.

Everything you do before you walk through that stage door—networking, writing a resume, getting references, researching employers—is merely preparation for your job tryout.

That "act" is real, though. But interviewers only know what you show. Use the techniques that follow to control the interview and show the interviewer—the director—what will inspire a hire.

This book contains the only acting lessons you need. By the time you've rehearsed them, you'll be ready to deliver your lines and leave with the part.

So—let's go on with the show!

1. Schedule for success.

I talked about timing of interviews in *Jeff Allen's Best: Get the Interview*. There's a reason for scheduling interviews according to this system—you maximize your control over them.

When you set up interviews in a random manner, there's a wide variance in your energy level, attention span, and response time. Winners in sports and almost every other human activity know that consistency gives them a competitive edge. Consistency in interviewing will give you the winner's edge, too. If you are out of work, set up two interviews a day, five days a week. One in the morning, around 9:00; the second in the afternoon, around 2:00.

You also want to strike a balance between *your* best time and the interviewer's. That's why it's helpful to know a few inside secrets.

In the first two books of this series I revealed what happens on Friday afternoons in a personnel office: "dehiring"—firings and exit interviews. If you're able to schedule an interview for Friday afternoon, however, that's probably not the case.

The closer you get to a weekend, the greater the chance your interview won't get full attention or be fully remembered. Monday mornings are hectic, too. New hires are being processed, responses from ads are flooding the phone or floor, and people aren't showing up for work. So, schedule your most crucial interviews for Monday afternoon through Thursday morning.

Another advantage of consistent scheduling is that you become accustomed to your own reactions when your body chemistry is in the same balance. This stabilizes your nervous system, enhances your confidence, and makes your delivery more consistent.

2. Limit interviews to 45 minutes.

The 45-minute time limit is critical. If the interview drags on beyond that, you will, too. You're not interviewing—you're *incarcerating*—imprisoning the interviewer. Say you have another appointment. You do. If you don't have one for another interview, it's for more scheduling. People always want what they can't have, or what they think someone else might get.

3. Avoid meal interviews.

Many qualified candidates fail their screen tests the minute they find their forks.

There's no way you can predict your interviewer's ingrained reactions to personal mannerisms, offhanded remarks, eating or drinking habits, and etiquette.

I'm not talking about obvious errors like using your knife as a spoon or as a slingshot. (I know it works well, but it must be cleaned with your shirt before you use it for a shoehorn.) One candidate was ruled out just because he salted his food. The *hiring executive's* blood pressure went up. He loudly refused to pay the bill and a food fight ensued. Only the local newspaper won: The restaurant critic wrote the incident up on the sports page.

With second interviews or for senior jobs, you may be *expected* to "enjoy" a meal with the hiring honchos. Avoid it if possible. If not, just be sure the "businessman's special" isn't *you*.

4. Eliminate fear of the unknown.

Just as an actor researches every character, you must prepare for playing your part. You probably got a jump on your homework during the *Get the Interview* phase of your search. Once you've arranged the interview, go back to the reference materials, your notes, and the phone to learn more about the company and the job.

Understanding the inner workings of each company you visit reduces your fear of the unknown, which directly increases the probability of winning the interview. As you develop a profile of each employer, you can reduce more than 90 percent of the mystery of the interview. From the time you walk through the stage door, your confidence will shine through.

These are all the sources I listed in *Get the Interview*:

Business Periodicals Index (H. W. Wilson Company)
Dictionary of Occupational Titles
Directory of Corporate Affiliations
Directory of Executive Recruiters
Dun and Bradstreet's Million-Dollar Directory
F&S Index of Corporations and Industries

Forbes: Annual Report of American Business

Forbes 500's

Fortune 500

MacRae's Blue Book

Moody's Manuals

Moody's News Reports

Standard Directory of Advertisers

Standard & Poor's Corporation Records

*Standard & Poor's Register of Corporations, Directors, and
    Executives*

Thomas Register of American Manufacturers

U.S. Bureau of Labor Statistics: Area Wage Surveys .

U.S. Industrial Product Directory

Value Line Investment Surveys

Wall Street Journal Index

100 Best Companies to Work for in America

Reviewing market shares, financial statements, and other statistics is fine for background. But, when it comes to winning the interview, understanding the employer's "corporate culture" is even more important. If you portray yourself as an autocratic manager when the company encourages "team decision making," you won't be offered anything but a parking validation.

Look up target employers in *The Reader's Guide to Periodical Literature* at your library. Check for recent magazine articles that describe the culture and philosophy.

With all the information available, don't let research detour the search. Just write brief notes on each company that will interview you, and review them a few times prior to your interview. The information will be stored in your brain, and it will pop out of your mouth at the right time during the interview. (Of course, that assumes nothing else is in the way at the time—so listen for the cue first.)

A faster, more enjoyable way to do jobsearch research, particularly if you're outgoing (or adventurous), is over the phone. It's also the fastest, most effective way to discover the *personality* of the organization. In a small organization, it may be the *only* way. So try a little behavioral modification for your telephobia. Call continuously until you become compulsive about it. Anonymously at first, if you like. Better compulsiveness than telephobia. It gets you hired.

No one's judging you—yet. Just reach out and touch (or even grab) someone in the sales department, marketing department, or public relations department. State the purpose of your call. Then sit back, lips zipped and ears open. You want to hear answers to questions like:

1. Where is the company headquartered?

2. Who owns the company?

3. How many locations does the company have? Where are they?

4. What divisions does the company have?

5. How many employees does the company have?

6. What are the main products or services of the company?

7. What markets does the company serve?

8. What are the future products or services of the company?

9. What are the annual sales of the company?

10. How long has the company been in operation?

Make copies of a worksheet with these questions (and space for the answers) to help you with your investigations. Even if you've never gathered market intelligence, after a little practice you'll crack any employer within a few minutes.

5. Complete an application in advance.

While you're making your phone calls, make one to the personnel receptionist to request a copy of the application. Arriving
with an application already neatly typed saves time, makes a
good impression, and guides you through the interview like a
road map. It also prevents you from fumbling, stumbling, and
mumbling into the interviewer's office.

6. Deputize internal referrals.

People like to talk about their jobs and their companies. Your
honesty in saying why you called, obvious interest, and appreciation may result in a bonus: an internal referral. Listen, but don't
lean. If you encounter a potential "inside agent," disclose who
you are and why you are calling. Mention that you would like to
introduce yourself when you're there. Remain passive. An aggressive approach could cause you to lose a valuable ally.

Finding an internal referral that you didn't know is one
example of interview leverage. When you get there, mention the
coworker's name. After the interview, call back the insider and
report on how it went. *Then* you can lean. If the person is
receptive, you can ask him or her to "put in a good word" for you
with the hiring authority.

Express your appreciation with a note and another call
around a week after the interview.

7. Dress the part and the part plays itself.

This is the rule every actor knows. First impressions *do* count.
But this is no time to make a fashion statement. Those who hire
are extremely busy and see many candidates. Standing out
because of your costume is definitely a way to be remembered—
and rejected. Know the uniform and wear it proudly.

John J. Molloy's New Dress for Success and *The Woman's Dress for Success Book*, both by John Molloy, are still the interview standards. In the former, Molloy wrote:

> Those of you who are . . . saying that fashion is an art form and not a science are making the same kind of statement as the eighteenth-century doctors who continued to bleed people. I do not contend that fashion is an absolute science, but I know that conscious and unconscious attitudes toward dress can be measured and that this measurement will aid men in making valid judgments about the way they dress.[1]

8.　The interviewing uniform for men.

This is the simplest step to winning the interview, because there *is* only one interview uniform for men. Tested over time, it still works consistently:

- *Dark (preferably Navy blue) conservative two-piece business suit.* Single-breasted. Any pattern should be subtle. Wool and wool blends look better and last longer. Have it custom tailored for the proper fit. When you look your best, you'll perform your best.

  Gray may be worn, but save it for the second interview. Lead with the dark blue suit, and you'll be more likely to be back in the gray one.

- *White, long-sleeved dress shirt.* Laundered and starched commercially. Wear a fresh one for each interview. Your interviewer won't wear a monogram, so you shouldn't. Collar style should be current; and, if French cuffs are worn, cuff links should not be too large or reflect any religious, fraternal, or service affiliation. They should also be the same finish as your watch.

- *Dark, striped tie.* Here, too, dark blue is best. A contrasting color (like red) is acceptable, but the predominant color should be the same as your suit. Silk or other thin fabrics are recommended.

- *Black dress shoes.* Almost any style is acceptable, as long as they can be polished well, and are. Check yours for needed repair work. If they're old or odd, replace them.

These four items comprise the all-American male look. Almost every image consultant agrees on its positive effect. I once appeared on a radio talk show with a famous designer who commented that when it comes to business wear, "men's fashion" is a contradiction in terms. There are no trends. Only tried and true (blue) tradition.

As for the rest of you (head and hands), your hair should be clean, neat, and conservatively cut. Keep any sprays or other hair dressings to an absolute minimum—no "wet look." Nails should be neatly trimmed. Leave diamond rings and any religious or organization jewelry at home. Your wedding band or school ring is acceptable.

9. The interviewing uniform for women.

Although there is far more interview fashion flexibility for women, important guidelines exist.

- *A conservative suit or dress* in a high-quality, dark-colored fabric is best. Navy and gray are rated high for sincerity. Brown and tan are not. Avoid high hemlines regardless of the current fad. Knee-length is the highest your hem should be.

  A suit should be paired with a business blouse or tailored shirt. While it doesn't have to have a "business bow," it shouldn't have a plunging neckline, either.

- *Shoes* should be simple, heels not too high, real leather in a dark color that matches or complements your clothes.

- *Hosiery* should be new, natural color or the color of your shoes.

- *Jewelry*, if worn, should be kept to a minimum. Good, simple gold and silver accessories are okay. (No jewelry should reflect any religious or organizational affiliation.) Flashy fashion jewelry is out.
- *Handbag* should not be too large, should be real leather, the color of your shoes, and in good condition. Don't stuff it until it bulges.

Women should show an awareness of current fashion, without being a slave to it. It will pay in the long run to invest in at least two well-coordinated interview uniforms. Your look should be conservative—even classic—but current.

Other rules:

- Don't wear much makeup or "mod" colors.
- Don't wear heavy perfume.
- Trim nails to an inconspicuous length and avoid bright nail polish colors. Invest in a professional manicure for the best look.
- Hair should be clean, shiny, and neatly and conservatively styled. Long hair should be pinned up or back. Curls cascading below your collar give the wrong impression.

There is increasing evidence that extremely attractive women are not hired as readily by men *or* women. Don't flaunt or you'll flunk.

10. Carry an attache case.

For both men and women, regardless of the position, a quality attache case is a necessity. It is businesslike and helps you identify with the interviewer. Dark brown and burgundy are the most popular colors, but I prefer black for men because it matches the shoes.

The case should be stocked neatly with a small container of instant coffee (I'm about to tell you why) or a few regular tea bags, mouthwash, deodorant, cologne, nonsmoking tablets (if necessary), a comb or brush, a gold pen with black ink, a legal pad, six extra copies of your resume, a completed application, and a few samples of your written or published work, if applicable.

11. Know the exceptions to the wardrobe rule.

These are few and far between. Highly creative art, fashion, and entertainment jobs are about the only places you'll find them. However, looking the part of the job you hope to find is far less effective than looking the part of the person who will hire you for it.

Even in fad and fashion industries, human resourcers still prefer a conservative look. They often make their decisions in committees—"clubs" consisting of other corporate clones. If you don't wear their middle-class and middle-management uniform, they'll think you belong with a rival gang.

Still, you can dress differently for an interview in such situations, if you know what the interviewer will be wearing. When in doubt, find out—by a phone call to a receptionist.

12. Fuel your jobgetting engine.

Remember the internal balance I talked about earlier in this section? In addition to the right timing and preparation, giving a good interview performance requires the right fuel. You should appear for an interview rested and relaxed.

I highly recommend coffee to keep you alert. Caffeine has a predictable, positive, harmless effect for interviewing purposes. It causes the neurons in the brain cells to fire faster. This actually helps you store and retrieve information readily. It's also a metabolism booster that raises your energy level. Both of these effects improve your delivery.

If coffee doesn't agree with you, try regular tea instead. It's less powerful, but has fewer side effects. Over-the-counter tablets should be avoided because their concentration of caffeine is higher or more dangerous drugs are used.

Eating a light snack about a half hour before the interview helps you avoid a stomach growl as you smile. It also prevents a sudden drop in your blood sugar level, which can make you snap or snore. The perfect snacks are those packages of cheese and peanut butter cracker sandwiches. They contain just the right proportions of carbohydrate, protein, and bulk. The salt reduces the diuretic effect of the coffee, so you won't have to leave for the restroom as the offer's being extended. Avoid fruit and candy; they accelerate the drop in blood sugar levels.

Pack a small bottle of red (cinnamon) mouthwash and use it. The zinc chloride-zinc oxide combination is much more effective much longer than any other type. Breath spray (even cinnamon) is far better to prevent the interviewer from attacking you. Then again, if you use breath spray, he or she probably won't get that close. Mints? They don't help bad breath and aren't even good ammo. Gum? Not if you want to get hired.

13. Arrive alone.

Remember this absolute rule of career success:

HE TRAVELS FASTEST WHO TRAVELS ALONE.

Violate it at your peril.

You may think you need moral support. That you'll survive if someone props you up. But you won't. Even a companion who waits for you in the reception area will reduce your chances of an offer by 80 percent. Think again.

You should also avoid attending any after-hours social meetings with a spouse or friend where an interviewer might be present.

Getting high-level jobs and ones where you entertain clients will sometimes require a second or third interview with your spouse. Usually the interviewer will invite you to dinner at a restaurant.

Now you're dealing with two problems. Rule 3 says "Avoid meal interviews." This rule says "Arrive alone." But if it's a requirement, you'll just have to go and hope for the best. Hope your companion behaves and is received well. Mention that he or she depends on you for support. Your companion should read these rules, too.

Eating encounters are tricky, treacherous, and too often terribly tragic. Recognize them as KO ("knockout") situations that screen candidates out rather than get them hired. They're only partially controllable, but if you must—do your best.

14. Arrive on time.

Don't arrive late. It demonstrates that you are neither time-conscious nor considerate.

If an emergency detains you, phone ahead to reschedule. Interviewers can understand traffic accidents, flat tires, and extended prior meetings. Just don't wait until the last minute to reschedule. Interviewers who wait don't scream, they screen.

The more important reason to avoid being late is that you must begin the appointment with an apology. This places you in a subordinate role and automatically turns your opening lines into a closing act. Do your apologizing, if at all, by telephone before you walk on the set.

15. Don't arrive early, either.

Arriving early is not better (or even the same) as arriving on time. When it comes to interviews, only fools rush in.

Another reason for not arriving early is that it pressures the interviewer. You don't want to increase the pressure on the interviewer. They have ways of dealing with you.

If you have allowed yourself adequate time for weather and traffic problems, encountered none, and therefore arrived *more than 20 minutes early* for your interview, don't enter through the personnel department and sit there reading. It will adversely affect your interview. That's one of the many reasons I recommend completing the application in advance.

16. Review your notes.

Last-minute "cramming" for the screen test will help you produce the responses you need when you need them.

Have that quick cup of coffee and snack. It will help you retain what you're reviewing.

17. Acclimate to your environment.

If you have 20 to 30 minutes before your interview, enter through the main doors, get your bearings, survey the premises, and read bulletin boards for information. Even in those companies where you're booked and kept in a holding cell until your interview time, ask, ask, *ask*. Learn about company history, philosophy, size, personality, employees, buzzwords, and events. It's a bonanza for an observant listener.

Just don't get involved in anything that will take more than a few minutes. With about 15 minutes to go, find the restroom and "rest." Close the door on the stall, sit down, close your eyes, take a deep breath, and relax. Imagine yourself winning the interview.

Then, get up, check yourself out in the mirror, freshen up, and practice your best smile.

Now, eyes forward, chin up, shoulders back, stomach in, feet straight, confident, self-assured, poised, suit brushed and breath fresh, check in with the receptionist, introduce yourself professionally, and state who you are there to see. Then, give the receptionist the neatly typed application.

If your appointment is with a department supervisor or other executive, the same technique applies. Only the application may not be necessary.

18. Don't wait more than a half hour for the interviewer.

Respect works two ways. If the interviewer is delaying on purpose just to get the upper hand, you'll have to call his or her bluff.

Even if it's an unavoidable, unintentional delay, you're better off not waiting. You'll be angry, irritable, and dropping from the psychomotor peak (helpful stage fright) reached at the scheduled time.

Politely tell the receptionist you cannot wait more than 15 minutes more. Be sure he or she tells the interviewer immediately.

If you choose to stay and see it through, consider it dress rehearsal. It is—you won't get hired.

19. Don't wear a coat, hat, or other outdoor clothing into the interview.

Remove any outerwear and hang it in the reception area. If no hangers are provided, ask the receptionist to hold it for you. Wearing a coat and hat into the interview psychologically separates you from the interviewer and physically requires dancing when you should be acting.

20. Don't wear sunglasses.

Sunglasses not only block the sun, they block your eyes. Direct eye contact is one of the most important techniques. Shades may be interpreted as "shady." Take dark glasses off as soon as you walk indoors, place them in your attache case, and don't wear them again until you're outside.

21. Have your script well rehearsed.

I told you earlier that your performance will be genuine. That's because you're going to write the script—and memorize it—in advance. A lawyer learns never to ask questions without knowing the answers. You must know the questions *and* learn the answers.

How? I've already said that the interview is a rehearsable, predictable, controllable event. You just need to script your answers in advance.

In *The Complete Q&A Job Interview Book*, I reviewed more than 250 questions to expect. They were each followed by a suggested, sometimes customized, answer. Then I showed how to organize the script and prepare the delivery for maximum effectiveness. In the next section I provide excerpts from *The Q&A Book* to get you started.

Don't skip rehearsals, or you'll find yourself center stage on a senseless rampage. You'll miss your cues and flub your lines. You won't get any parts.

Just keep reading—and remembering—and you *will* win, time and time again.

Chapter

2

The Script: Know the Answers in Advance

I've read almost every book on how to interview—took courses on it, led seminars about it, and even trained supervisors to do it. As I recalled in *The Complete Q&A Job Interview Book*:

> I rapped nonstop about interviewing techniques: "directive" or "nondirective," "specific" or "general," "closed ended" or "open ended," "structured" or "unstructured," "restricted" or "unrestricted," "window," "choice," "hypothetical," "theoretical," "interpretive," "leading," "loaded," "stress," "interrogation," "machine-gun," "multiple," "double," "curiosity" . . .
>
> It's a welcome break for supervisors and keeps a lot of personnelers off the unemployment line. But studying interviewing techniques [used by personnel types] is a total waste of time for a serious jobseeker. At best, studying it will get you tired long before you're hired. At worst, it will intimidate you. Interviewing hasn't changed since Laurel hired Hardy. It's just as comical as it has always been.[2]

22. Use the "programmed interview system" to fast-forward your future.

It maximizes the positive impact of the "actor factor." You can memorize the script in advance, by using a technique I taught in *The Q&A Book*. It's called the programmed interview system—and it works.

At first, most people are afraid they'll respond like a bionic with a broken brain, and just talk or move out of context. Not a chance. The subconscious just stores. Words and actions then happen naturally when the time is right.

Follow the steps given here, and the interviewer will never know you're using the system. He or she won't care, either. He or she wants that job requisition off his or her desk and out of his or her life for as long as possible. Show a glimmer of star quality and some indication that you know your lines, and he or she will even coach you for the part.

Oh, maybe you have some "moral" problems with using the "actor factor" to your advantage and not "being yourself." If so, I suggest you ask a past interviewer for the rating forms he or she used on you. It won't get you hired, but it will open your eyes wide to the games interviewers play, and how biased, unfair, and incorrect their snap judgments really are. Now, you can work this to your advantage.

People who interview well are better employees, too. That's because they have learned how to interact on the job—to sell themselves and their ideas to others. They aren't enslaved because they know they can always find another job. They're working because they *want* to.

Programmed interviewing teaches the kind of positive interacting skill that gets people hired, promoted, and recruited for better opportunities elsewhere. By using this system, you are taking the most random selection process imaginable and controlling it.

That's right—you are in control. No, you won't be switching seats with the interviewer—you'll never have that much control. It's his or her office and decision (almost). After all, he or she can always yell "Cut!"

So don't fight it. Just *do* it. Let it work for you. Then you won't want to fight it anyway. You'll feel great about yourself when you know you can knock any interview cold. You should. You have lifetime employment insurance and a supercharged career.

Highlights of the programmed interview system follow in this section. Follow the next six steps to fast-forward your future.

23. Scan the script.

Read the questions and answers to yourself once.

24. Customize it to the target job.

Customize the questions where necessary to conform to the ones you'll be asked.

25. Customize it to your "character."

Customize the answers where necessary to your vocabulary and way of speaking. (Just don't change it radically; each answer is carefully designed and tested to score the most points. The further you deviate from it, the more you risk.)

26. Record and replay.

Prepare a cassette for yourself containing the most difficult questions for you to answer, leaving spaces on the tape to read your answers aloud.

    You can stop the tape occasionally to rehearse a particular response, but it is important to simulate an interview where the dialogue continues. Remember, no retake in that personnel playhouse.

27. Rehearse your delivery.

Play the cassette at least three times a week for the next two weeks, sitting in front of a full-length mirror. Make an interviewing "set" by using a table for a desk and adding other props. Pay attention to your facial expressions, hand movements, and body language. Smile. Look the "interviewer" (you) in the eye. Try not to speak with your hands. Lean forward to make a point.

If you want to learn more about how body language can be used most effectively, pick up the paperbacks *Contact: The First Four Minutes* by Leonard Zunin and *Body Language* by Julius Fast.

28. Repeat it 'till it rolls off your tongue.

Use your driving, riding, or walking time to listen to the cassette and answer the questions.

You can just *think* the answers, but talking aloud to an imagined interviewer will rivet your attention. Engaging your mouth when your brain is in gear is good practice.

29. Personal questions: Know the knockout factors.

Of all the categories of questions you will be asked, those pertaining to your personal and family life seem to be the most "statistical." As a result, most jobseekers answer them in a "static" way, providing only the basic information: name, rank, and serial number.

These questions are often emotionally charged, since they delve into personal perils, family feuds, and status symbols. Therefore, rehearsing your lines in this area is particularly important, because what you *say* is as crucial as what you *convey*.

While most of the questions in this area have only marginal value in determining your qualifications to perform a specific job, you must get past them so that you can get down to business with the interviewer. That is why they are called "KO factors" (knockout factors). Wrong answers will knock you out in Round 1; right ones will keep you in the ring like Rocky.

Personal and family items are commonly found on the front of application forms, and at the beginning of interview checklists. Because you can expect these questions early in the screen test, I have provided your cue cards early in this section.

SCRIPT

Q.   What is your father's occupation? Your mother's?

(Think your answer through. Avoid saying anything negative like, "My father was just a janitor," or "My mother didn't work." Show pride in your background and heritage, even if you regard it as very humble. "My father was a custodial supervisor, and my mother ran a busy home" is more positive.

Be careful about overstating, too. Avoid an answer like "My father is the leading brain surgeon in the state and my mother is a retired Superior Court judge." In such cases, "My father is a surgeon and my mother is an attorney and former judge" positions you properly.)

A.   My father is a _____ and my mother is a _____ .

Q.   Do you live with your parents?

(It's okay if you do. Even mature adults are finding it financially beneficial to share expenses with their parents. Give the impression that you made a responsible financial decision.)

A.   Yes, I moved back in with my parents after I discovered that over half my net income was being used to pay for rent and utilities. We have an economic arrangement that allows me to save for my future, while I'm around to help them maintain our home. We all benefit, and we have been able to develop a strong friendship as three adults.

Q.   Were you in the military service? Where and when?

(If yes, give dates and where stationed. Mention briefly any training or experience that relates directly to the target position.)

A.   I served as a _____ in the _____ from _____ to _____ .

Q.   Do you own or rent your home?

(This is one of those questions that attempts to establish your stability. The translation is, "Are you a responsible member of the community?" Answer briefly and honestly. If you are renting while you save to buy your own home, mention where you've been looking. If you haven't, start now with a call to a local real estate agent.)

A.   (I/we) purchased our home in _____ (name of town) in _____ (year).

(Or:)

   (I am/we are) currently renting a (house/unit) in _____ (name of town), but (I'm/we're) looking for (my/our) own home in the area.

Q.   How far do you live from this company?

(If you currently live farther away than what would be considered a reasonable commuting distance, you might mention you would be willing to locate nearer the company's offices if hired.)

A.   I clocked it on my way here today. I'm exactly 10 miles door to door, and it took me 17 minutes to get here. A breeze.

(Or:)

   The ride here today was 40 miles, and with moderate traffic it took almost an hour. I don't mind commuting that far twice a day—I like to get an early start on my day anyway. If I were hired, however, I would probably investigate the real estate market in the immediate area.

Q.   Do you speak a foreign language?

(If you speak another language fluently, by all means say so. This is an asset. However, if you took Spanish or French in school but cannot remember more than two or three phrases, simply mention that you understand the language better than you speak it. Try this answer:)

A.   I studied _____ (Spanish/French/German) in

_____ (high school/college) and enjoyed it. I'd like to get some language tapes and increase my fluency.

Q. How much time do you spend with your family?

(Be careful to project a balanced attitude here. This can be a touchy subject. You may be dealing with an interviewer who is work-oriented and lives by the credo, "Work is not only the way to make a living, it's the way to make a life." Or, you may be talking to one who recognizes the importance of a family. Before you answer, scope out the situation: Look around the office for family photos, desk accessories made by children, and the like. The following is your basic "generic" answer. Customize it as necessary.)

A. I suppose I spend an average amount. My family is important to me. My great relationship with them gives me the best reason in the world to succeed in my career. In that way, they are an inspiration.

I have a responsibility to my job as well as to my family, since I've made a strong commitment to both. I like to be there for them when they need me, but they also understand and accept the commitment I have made to my work. So I spend my time accordingly.

Q. Is your spouse employed? Will there be a conflict?

(This is one of those logical but unnecessary questions that is often asked. If you answer it in a neutral way, the interviewer will go on to something else. But if you indicate there is a conflict, it could reduce your chances of being hired. The following answer usually works well.)

A. Yes, my _____ (husband/wife) is a _____ (computer programmer/astronaut) for _____. We have always been a two-career couple, and we have made the arrangements necessary to accommodate our careers.

Q. What child care arrangements have been made for your children?

(While this question was rarely, if ever, asked of a male applicant in the past, it is and should be an employer's concern no matter who is applying for the job. Over half the children in America today are being raised by single heads of household or have two working parents, and the lack of quality child care is a problem that can intrude upon any parent's work life. Letting the interviewer know you have worked out a solid solution will show your sense of responsibility to those important people in your life, as well as to your work.)

A.   Our children attend an excellent nursery school and day care center near our home. The youngest is there all day, and the oldest is dropped off after school. Usually, my _____ (husband/wife) picks them up at night, while I have responsibility for morning drop-off. If work commitments prevent both of us from getting there by six, when they close, there is a responsible neighbor who picks them up, brings them home, and prepares dinner for them.

Q.   Have you any chronic health conditions we should consider?

(If not, then simply answer, "No." The question is illegal, and the interviewer is asking for your opinion. The only time you should answer this question positively is if you do have a condition that will become evident in a pre-employment physical, like diabetes. In that case, you might answer:)

A.   Nothing that would interfere with my work performance. I have had diabetes for ____ years, but I control it very successfully and unobtrusively. It has never become an issue in my work; and, aside from my family, only my doctor knows. It isn't a secret—it just has nothing to do with performing the job.

30.   Educational background questions: Show what you know.

Although not as sensitive an area as questions relating to personal and family data, educational background questions still can cause applicants to trip when they make their grand entrance.

Degree delirium reached epidemic proportions in the United States during the 1960s and 1970s. After many casualties (and fatalities) American industry seems to be realizing that experience in thinking does not necessarily correlate to ability at doing. Experience at doing is a much more accurate predictor of job performance. If you doubt this, just view the early films of most veteran actors.

I discussed the value of initials after your name in *Finding the Right Job at Midlife*:

> During a recent tour, I found myself in front of a microphone on an all-night radio talk show somewhere west of New York. I ran out of fingers counting the number of interviews that day, and was due to catch a plane to the next city. Since they're so much easier to catch when they're on the ground, the host announced that the next call would be the last. The caller asked, "What does the 'J.D., C.P.C.' after your name mean?" Of course, the straight answer would have been, "Juris Doctor and Certified Placement Counselor." But I just couldn't be straight under the circumstances. As I removed the headset and stood up to leave, my candid reply said it all: "The 'J.D.' stands for 'Just Do It!', and the 'C.P.C.' stands for 'Courage, Persistence and Confidence'!"[3]

So unless you're applying for a job that requires completion of a specialized course of study for entry (lawyer, doctor, certified public accountant, etc.), don't waste a good worry about that piece of paper. In fact, be careful about accentuating unrelated education—it can pull you off the stage like a hook from the wings.

Don't falsify anything, and be sure to indicate any other names you used in school. Educational records are easily checked, and usually are.

Instead, sell how your education ties in with:

- *A business approach.*
- *Self-discipline.*
- *The target job.*

SCRIPT

Q.   What college did you attend?

A.   I went to _____ in _____ .

Q.   Why did you attend that particular college?

A.   I chose _____ because of its competitive atmosphere and the good reputation of the _____ School. Although I could have attended other colleges, this one emphasized practical, job-related courses and student participation in activities related to their specific careers.

Many of my friends found themselves going to colleges their parents had chosen, but I set my own educational and career goals. _____ may have been a little more expensive than some of the other colleges, but this forced me to work harder since I helped pay my own way.

I'm pleased with my decision. I relied on my instincts, and they paid off. Now, I'm extremely optimistic about my future, since my college education also taught me self-reliance, time management, and the value of hard work.

Q.   Did your family have any influence on your choice of college?

A.   My family had several suggestions to make, but they realized I was pretty sure of myself and knew what I wanted. They stood back and let me decide. They agreed with my decision when I shared the results of my research with them.

Q.   What made you choose _____ as your major?

(Your answer here will obviously depend on your individual situation. Here are two scripted responses. The first is for people who majored in a subject or area that directly applies to their careers. The second is for those who majored in one thing and are doing another.)

A. I always knew _____ (business management/ electrical engineering) was where I had the most potential, and I've remained with it because I turned out to be right. Not everyone is as fortunate as I have been. It's very difficult at 18 to predict and plan for the future; but, even then, I knew what I wanted to do. I'm glad I set my goals at a young age. It has worked out well for me.

(Or:)

At the age of 18 nothing in the world seemed so important as _____ (American history/philosophy/English literature) and I studied for the sake of learning. Later, I realized I needed further education in subjects that would help me in my career.

Q. Do you feel you made the right choice?

(Again, the first answer is for those who never made a career veer, and the second is for the rest of the world.)

A. Absolutely. And my career success bears me out. I am very happy with the path my life and work have followed.

(Or:)

Yes, at the time I did. I learned a great deal, and I believe in the value of education. I of course went on to learn more, both formally and on the job, that applies directly to my field. I'm glad I started out in one area and switched to another. It has enhanced my ability to be creative and flexible, since I have learned different approaches to performing the work successfully.

Q. How have your education and training prepared you for the job?

A. My education gave me the tools to succeed and my training taught me how to do the job properly. Before I really knew what my job entailed, I only thought I would perform it well.

The training gave me the opportunity to apply my education. By having the chance to do the work expected of me in advance, I gained the confidence to meet future challenges and the experience to do so successfully. The real challenge starts where the education and training end.

Studying diligently and practicing constantly really paid off. Now I am confident in my work and have earned the respect of my coworkers.

Q. Why didn't you continue your formal education?

A. Two reasons. The first was my impatience to earn rather than learn. The second reason was that I enjoyed being productive. As I mentioned, I worked part time to pay my college expenses, and I was fortunate to be employed by some excellent companies.

My employers always seemed to want more of my time and talents. And in many cases I was working at levels way beyond what I was studying in my classes. Finally, I left school in my _____ year and devoted myself full time to my career. I've never regretted that decision, because I have continued to learn and grow with my work.

Q. Are you currently taking, or do you plan to take, any evening courses?

A. I am presently studying _____ at _____, which I find very valuable to my ongoing job performance and general knowledge.

(Or:)

With the demands of keeping up with my job while interviewing, I haven't signed up for anything this semester, but as soon as I've made a decision and settled into my new position, I'm sure I'll be looking at those catalogues again. There's always something being offered that can help me perform better and bring new ideas to my work. I like to learn about new developments. Education is a lifelong process.

Q. What are your educational goals for the future?

A. My goal is to do everything possible to keep learning and improving. Things change so rapidly that we cannot rely on what we learned ten, five, even two years ago. Some of my education will be informal: reading, research, and simply paying attention to what is going on. You can learn a lot just by listening to the right people, and watching them.

(If applicable:)

Also, however, I _____ (am taking/ plan to take) courses in _____ at _____ (name of school) and hope to complete a (bachelor of _____/master of _____) by _____ (date).

Q. Did your grade point average reflect your work ability?

A.   My grades were above average to excellent, and I think my work record has been the same. There is a different method of evaluation in school, of course, and I've worked harder on the job than I did in school. At work, it's results that count, and I've always been able to achieve results. It's not just what you know, but what you do with what you know. This has always been my formula for career success.

(Or:)

I earned average grades in school, but my work record has been good to excellent. In school you are evaluated simply by how well you show what you know. At work, it's what you do with what you know—the results you achieve—that counts for everything. I've always concentrated on the result, and I've always delivered.

Q. Name three things you learned in school that could be used on this job.

A.   There are many specific applications to this field that I studied in school, including _____, _____, and _____. But what school really taught me that has worked throughout my career was how to solve problems, how to apply myself, and finally, how to set a goal and achieve it.

Q. Why didn't you do better in school?

A.   I guess I was just involved with other activities and growing up. I always got along with my teachers and classmates, and even won awards for _____ (perfect attendance/science projects/and so forth). The importance of grades did not have an impact on me then. Today I realize the value of formal academic achievement, and my "career marks" have always been well above average.

31. Character questions: Be careful!

"Character" is the most subjective area of all. Your "personality" probably changed several times today *alone*.

But the interviewer will try to take a reading on your character with the type of questions that follow. Rehearse this part of the script especially well, so you don't flub your lines or reveal any quirks and eccentricities that will make the director think "Cut!" and reject you as a candidate.

When you become a pro at interviewing, you have an advantage even professional actors don't have. You can schedule the best time for you. Thus, you stage-manage the character that the interviewer sees. Being a good stage manager dramatically affects your delivery. You'll be surprised at how your appearance, posture, attitude, reaction time, and overall confidence improve.

So much for "character traits."

SCRIPT

Q. Do you consider yourself to be a smart person?

A.   Yes. That means I'm smart enough to know my opinion is biased. The kind of intelligence required on the job isn't always measured by an IQ test. Only through coping with different situations and interacting with other people can intelligence truly be judged. By these criteria, I'm above average in intelligence.

When it comes to working with people, solving business problems, and making decisions—especially those related to the job—I'm as good as or better than anyone else. There are many things I don't know, but I can learn. In that way, a smart person is one who asks questions, listens carefully, and realizes nobody knows everything.

Q. How important is job security to you?

A. Security is a basic need, but I know that there are no guarantees in life. The only true job security comes from making a meaningful contribution to my employer. If I know my job will be around for as long as I excel at it, I am able to concentrate on my work and remain focused. The best environment is one where employer and employee form a partnership for their mutual benefit.

The first priority of any job is the work itself. Everything else is secondary. As long as I find myself challenged by my work and am respected by those around me, I'm confident that I'll be able to continue getting the work done properly, always meeting or exceeding expectations.

Q. What are the reasons for your success?

A. I always give a hundred percent. Some people try to prove themselves to someone else, but I think sometimes it's better to prove to yourself that you can succeed. No one is a better judge of your success than you, and you know what you can do. When I do a job well, it gives me personal satisfaction that carries over into everything I do.

Although I work very hard, I find that I get along with all sorts of people. By respecting everyone as an individual as you advance in responsibility, you not only make a good impression but you also gain the respect of others.

Paying attention to details is also important. I usually like to recheck everything I do, just in case I missed something the first time. I also find it beneficial to at least review any work that has my name on it, even if completed by a secretary or someone else in my department. Proper delegation requires some supervision.

Eventually, hard work, respect for others, and attention to detail pay off, and they make the job more enjoyable and challenging along the way.

Q.   Do you like to work with "things?"

(If yes, or if the job requires manual, technical aptitude:)

A.   Yes, I've always had an aptitude for the absolute and definable. I have good technical ability and can "make things work." I have the ability, however, to conceptualize a job and then translate those concepts into reality.

(If no, or if the job is more conceptual in nature:)

Yes, but usually as the result of design and concept. This work takes ideas, imagination, and the ability to formulate a project from beginning to end—see it first, then specify what it will take for others to make it work. I'm the idea person, but I pride myself on being a practical realist. An idea is only as good as its use.

Q.   Do you like to work with facts and figures?

(If yes, or if job requires analytical and math skills:)

A.   Absolutely. That's the basis of this work. I've always had a flair for the numbers side of the business, and my thought processes are very analytical and precise. Accurate books and records are an essential management tool, and can help to identify areas that need improvement.

(If no, or the job likely would not fit the thinker/analyzer personality:)

A.   Facts and figures are important. I respect them, I'm good with them, but I don't get bogged down in them. I always read the reports, and I'm quick to spot inconsistencies and errors. I don't check every number twice, though, because that's not what produces results. Financial records are like X-rays that allow a doctor to make a diagnosis. I leave the preparation to the skilled technicians.

Q.   Do you like to work with people?

(If yes, or if it's a teamwork situation:)

A.   Without a doubt. If we're to meet our goals and keep up with the growth that's predicted for this industry, we'll have to organize and coordinate the efforts of many people. There's a *synergy* in teamwork that can accomplish far more than the same individuals could working alone. When a group of people is working together, there's nothing like it. The energy and creativity we activate in each other are many times greater. The whole is greater than the sum of its parts.

(If the job requires solitary hours analyzing reports or crunching numbers:)

I've always worked well with others, but I have no difficulty getting my work done independently. I'm a self starter, can set my goals, or take assigned goals and complete them. I'm comfortable with myself.

Q.   Are you absent from work often?

(If your work record shows extended absence as the result of an injury or illness that is no longer a factor, explain what happened and why it no longer affects your attendance. Otherwise, use the following:)

A.   No, my attendance record is very good. I think you'll see when you check that the few days I missed work were due to the usual flu viruses going around. I figure, when you're sick, it's better to take off one day and get well rather than going to the office, working at half speed, and taking off more time to recuperate. I'd rather work at home when I'm sick than expose coworkers to my illness.

I'm in good health and rebound quickly. I've noticed that people who miss a lot of work really don't like their jobs or themselves very well.

Q.   How do you show your interest in your coworkers?

A.   By keeping my eyes and ears open. I try to be sensitive to those around me. If someone behaves in a way that is different from what I expect, I ask myself, "Why? Are there problems that have caused this person to perform differently?"

On a day-to-day basis, I try to remember the little things that are important to the people around me. I follow up and ask them how things are going without becoming overbearing. Work teams often become like a family, and it's important to remember that coworkers need to be appreciated, liked, and respected.

If I am the supervisor in the relationship, I usually call a quick, closed-door conference to see if there's something that can be done before a possible problem becomes a probable one.

Q.   Do you have any fear that may deter you from traveling by air?

(If you have an enduring phobia that prevents you from traveling by air, you shouldn't be applying for an astronaut's job. Go for what you know and like.)

A.   None at all. I've always recognized the speed of air travel as necessary to business, and I've traveled routinely in past jobs. The most important thing is to get in front of the customer so I can make the sale (solve the problem), and I view it as all in a day's (or night's) work.

Q.   What would you do if it were your last day on Earth?

A.   That's a tough question, but not as tough as having it happen! I'd gather the people who are important to me, and really let them know how much they've contributed to my happiness. I've led a fulfilling life, and enjoy what I do every day. The book can close on anyone at any time. That's why it's important to live it a page at a time.

Q.   Name three books you've read in the past six months.

(Don't mention any of mine—your secret's safe with me! Keep your eye on the business bestseller list, and mention three current titles. Management-oriented ones give you the highest marks.)

A.   Let's see. I really enjoyed _____ (*Managing for Excellence*), and on a holiday ski trip I took along _____ (*The One-Minute Manager*), which I found very revealing. Then, on the plane here I finally got to read _____ (*Executive Essentials*), which had been in my briefcase for a while.

Q.   Do you have a competitive nature?

A.   Yes. A competitive nature is necessary to be successful in a corporate environment. But competitiveness doesn't mean vying with my coworkers for recognition, raises, or promotions. If I do my work well and always give my best effort, the rewards will come. I've found that's the only real way to succeed.

But I do compete with myself. I'm always trying to break my own record—to do something better or faster than I did it the last time. I'm especially competitive when it comes to improving my company's product or service.

There's so much potential for accomplishment when you're part of a vibrant company like this one.

32.   Initiative and creativity questions: Focus on what and why.

Have you ever noticed how much "initiative" you have when you're uncomfortable? You're also highly creative in devising ways to bring yourself back into your comfort zone. The more you itch, the more you scratch.

For interviewing purposes, concentrate on the parts of former jobs that you improved. Then work backwards. . . . If "necessity is the mother of invention," then "invention is the daughter of necessity." Focus on what you did, then why.

Next, tie these improvements into the target job. You'll be surprised how easy this is, since initiative and creativity are highly transferable. Once you learn how to scratch, it doesn't matter where you itch.

Scratch out your script using the following questions as a guide.

SCRIPT

Q. What do you do when you have trouble solving a problem?

A.   One thing I don't do is ignore it and hope it will go away. I'm not afraid to ask questions or look for the answers myself. There is a solution to every problem. Sometimes, it just takes creative investigation. I'm a problem solver by nature. Nothing puzzles me for long—if it does, I just keep working until I find the solution.

Q. What have you done in your present job to make it more effective or more challenging?

A.   I've made my job more effective by finding ways to stream-line the paperwork and administration so that I can focus more effort and energy on producing results. Working smarter and harder really accomplishes a lot.
     More challenging? I'm always looking for new opportunities, and I've been particularly successful in finding different applications for the existing product and its users. I _____
_____
_____ .
(Mention briefly an example of using initiative and creativity to help the company, such as "found a new market for the XYZ product among _____"; or "saw a problem with the computer system and recommended _____," or something similar.)

Q. What is the most boring job you've ever had? How did you do at it?

A.   I haven't found any of my work in my adult career "boring." I've always been too busy to be bored!

Perhaps, as a teenager, you could say I wasn't very excited about some of the part-time work available. But I always found something positive about every job. When I was behind the counter at a fast-food store selling 1,000 hamburgers a day, the routine was eased by the hundreds of people I met. There has been something interesting, something that held my attention, about every job I've held, or I don't think I would have taken the job in the first place.

Q. What is the most interesting job you've ever had? How did you do at it?

A. My most interesting job to date has been _____ _____, because of _____ _____. I received particularly favorable performance reviews in that job, but I've had excellent ratings in all my work. When I make a commitment to a job, I give it all I've got.

Q. Is there a lot of pressure in your present job? How do you cope with it?

A. There is pressure in every job. In my present job, the pressure is usually associated with production deadlines or special projects. Experience has taught me how to cope with pressure.

All jobs have more demands at some times than others. The key is to manage your time and prioritize the work so you're ready for anything. When I work out the details and set the schedule in advance, I see that any big job can be broken down into many smaller jobs. When taken one at a time, any task can be mastered.

I respond to pressure, I don't react to it. After analyzing the components of a project, I take a few steps back so I can see the "big picture." This approach has seen me through many a tough situation with results that exceeded what anyone imagined— except perhaps me.

Q. What do you think it takes for a person to be successful in _____ (specialty of position being

discussed, such as engineering, parts assembly, customer service)?

A.   I think you need good skills in _____

_____ (conceptualizing a design/working with your hands/dealing with people).

In addition, being successful in this work requires a drive to do your best, and to continually improve on your past performance. One reason I think I've succeeded is that my past accomplishments have given me self-confidence. I view each day and each task as a new challenge, and an opportunity for improvement on whatever I did yesterday. Knowing that yesterday was successful helps me approach today and tomorrow with a "can-do" attitude. After all, I did do!

Q.   How do you go about making important decisions?

A.   I evaluate my options, laying them all out in front of me. I find it helps to write down briefly what my alternatives are, so I can examine them objectively. Then I rely on past experience, company policies, and—in part—intuition to guide me to a decision. I look at each situation individually, and weigh possible outcomes before making a choice.

If it is a big decision that has no precedent, I get input from those who will be affected by it—the staff—as well as those who will be called upon to explain my decision—my superiors.

Q.   Has anyone in the business world been an inspiration to you?

A.   Yes, several people. I've been fortunate to work with bright, talented, energetic individuals. Several of my managers have served as informal mentors who helped me develop my own management skills and style.

In every field, the trainees learn from the pros. I've never been so sure of my abilities that I wasn't willing to listen and learn from those who had more experience and had accomplished more. I think I've learned an even greater amount from these individuals than from the textbooks I've read and courses I've taken.

Q. Are you able to work alone without direct supervision?

A. Definitely. I'm a self-starter and finisher. I usually only need direction once—the first time I do something—and from then on I work well on my own. I'm inner-directed and enjoy applying my creativity and problem-solving skills to my work.

However, I'm not one of those individuals who will keep doing something wrong rather than getting help out of some fear of "looking bad." If I'm not sure about a task, or whether I'm getting the expected results, I check with the person in charge to make sure. I'm not afraid to ask questions.

I don't believe in that old saying, "'Tis better to remain silent and be thought a fool than to open your mouth and remove any doubt." I much prefer, "It doesn't matter who is right, but what is right." The important thing is to do the job right, and with the greatest efficiency and productivity.

Q. How did you handle the toughest decision you ever had to make?

A. I remember it well. I had to _____ (make a decision that would affect the jobs of several employees, perhaps requiring permanent layoffs). I thought seriously about the consequences to the employer without ignoring the human factors involved. I arrived at a solution that produced the best result for the company while minimizing the effects on the employees.

We kept the most qualified people, but those who had to leave were good employees also. We were able to help each one of them get work in the same field within a month of leaving our company. That minimized our unemployment insurance burden and kept those who were affected by the downsizing from losing self-esteem.

Making the right decision required a lot of forethought and looking at best- and worst-case scenarios extensively before making my recommendations. I firmly believe you have to look carefully at both the business and the people side of every work decision.

33. Questions about management ability: You're an "MBA."

That stands for "Most Believable Applicant." And you will be, when you master the questions that follow.

Since the ability to manage depends on sustained personal interaction with subordinates, it's virtually impossible for your "skill" to be measured. Interviews aren't held with understudies present.

The closest an interviewer can get is to find out whether you've learned how to apply basic principles. Asking you about "results" is about as reliable as asking an actor whether he deserves an Oscar.

What if you've never managed anyone? Not to worry. Just sensitize yourself to situations where you supervised others. It doesn't have to be a cast of thousands. Be ready to discuss how you helped organize them to accomplish specific tasks.

If the tasks aren't job related, aim for anything that's business-related. Even charity fund-raising and community service projects can be effectively woven into the script. Managing a dozen volunteers can be the equivalent of directing a cast of hundreds.

Your local public library stocks many books and periodicals on management. A few current ones are all you need to pick up theory, the latest buzzwords, or an interesting case study.

SCRIPT

Q. As a department manager, how would you go about establishing rapport with your staff?

A. I would first want to know as much about each individual

as I could, professionally as well as personally. Every employee is an individual and cannot be evaluated solely by arbitrary standards. Independent judgment is the major part of every manager's job, and there can be several "right" ways to approach something.

By reviewing each individual's position and work record, I would gain insight about his or her strong points and weaknesses. Similarly, by meeting with each person on a one-to-one basis and making myself open to candid dialogue, the stage would be set for a healthy working relationship.

Too many supervisor-subordinate relationships are like two monologues rather than one dialogue. This is a management problem, and a manager's responsibility to solve. In a word, I'd start by listening.

Q. What makes the best manager?

A. The best manager is a person dedicated to company goals while remaining sensitive to the individual uniqueness of each employee he or she manages. Managing people effectively is a difficult job, but the rewards in helping them develop while contributing to company objectives are great.

Essentially, good management requires understanding human nature so that you can motivate people to fulfill their potential. The best manager develops people to their fullest. He or she creates a system that allows the department to operate so efficiently that the work won't skip a beat if he or she isn't there, and also allows for smooth succession if he or she is promoted.

Exciting and igniting people is the manager's vision.

Q. What do your subordinates think are your strengths?

A. The people who have worked for me will tell you I am fair and I have a balanced approach to managing that considers both the business and people side of every issue. They know I don't make decisions in haste that everyone will repent at leisure. And, working for me usually means being on a winning team, where the coach expects everyone to give 110 percent. I ask a lot, but they love it.

Q. What do your subordinates think are your weaknesses?

A. What might be perceived by some as "weaknesses" are really my strengths. I expect a lot from my staff, but no more than I expect from myself. I look for and reward people who show initiative and creativity.

People I've supervised in the past will tell you that they worked harder in my department than in any other job. They'll also tell you they enjoyed it more, because they were accomplishing more.

Q. Tell me about the people you hired in your (present/last) job. How long did they stay with you? How did they work out?

A. I've developed a sense of the type of employee who will do a particular job well, and also a sense of what people work best together in a given situation, so there's always been a minimum of unrest and turnover among the troops.

I think any manager's best bet is to be candid right from the start. I don't overstate or oversell the job, but I let prospective employees know we value their contribution. I also let them know what I expect and what the job entails. It's important to get the right person for the job, or both the person and the job suffer.

Once you hire people, you must take the time to train them properly and give them the tools they need to do the job right. Then you determine who will work best with a minimum of guidance, and who needs more supervision. Management is like a dance, where you anticipate the music to stay in step. It doesn't have to cause corporate musical chairs.

Q. What are some of the things your (current/previous) employer might have done to be more successful?

A. I don't overanalyze the reasons for management decisions. Any decision is only as good as the facts upon which it is based. Management has access to market research, projections, and other important data. Yet, sometimes, even with the best input, things don't work out. Overall, the companies I've worked for have been very sound and I learned a great deal from their successes as well as their failures. In fact, the failures can be the reasons for the successes!

Q. In what manner do you communicate with staff? With superiors?

A. In most cases, a manager must develop a uniform and consistent communication style, so employees know what to expect. I would say I project assertiveness and a positive attitude when communicating with my staff, but I'm also flexible.

Good managers are skilled in the art of communication, and sensitive to the different personality styles of their employees. With some, you adapt a more outgoing style; with others you must be reserved and careful or they will feel threatened. There are cues and constant feedback from the subordinate. A good manager knows how to read these and respond properly.

You develop communication skill by listening, not just hearing. It becomes second nature to adapt your own style to that of the person with whom you are speaking. This is the fastest way to get on the same wavelength and avoid misunderstanding. It takes a little more effort on the manager's part, but I've seen the results and they are definitely worth it. Management theorists call this "pacing." You need to align with someone before you can lead him or her.

When acting as the communications link between your staff and superiors, representing your department to upper management and upper management to your department, the best communication style is one that is open, honest, and allows others the freedom to question.

Much of the success in the corporate environment depends on clear communication of company goals and directions—and listening to feedback. Fostering good communication is one of my top priorities.

Q. What steps would you take to terminate an employee who is not performing adequately?

A. First, I'd make sure I followed all applicable company rules and procedures, and any laws that govern the given situation.

People should have at least one warning, and a chance to improve their performance. I would counsel confidentially and give a written warning covering a specific period of time, along with clear guidelines for improvement. Then I would watch carefully and be sure to acknowledge and praise the employee for a sincere effort to remedy the situation.

However, if counseling and warning fail to produce results, I would not hesitate to terminate the employee. Firing is probably the hardest thing a manager does, because you come to know your employees as people. But, when someone who is notified that his or her work is below acceptable standards won't take steps to save his or her own job, the manager must protect the company. Again, I would make sure my actions were properly documented and that justifiable cause for termination was shown.

Q. What plan of action do you take when facing a problem?

A. Before I act, I think. I try to distance myself from the problem so that I can look at it objectively and analyze all sides. Sometimes I even write it down to see it more clearly.

When I've reached a decision, I present my planned solution to the people affected by it or those who must carry it out. I get their input, incorporate any suggestions that are appropriate, and then we implement the plan.

I believe in immediate but realistic solutions to problems. Ignoring them rarely makes them go away.

Q. (Did/Does) your staff come to you with personal problems?

A. My staff knows my door is always open, but they also know my number-one priority is getting the job done right and on time. They have come to me with personal problems in the past only when those personal problems might interfere with work progress. I have shown sympathy, but my advice and solutions have always been offered with the company's goals in mind.

Q. (Did/Do) you run your department only "by the book?"

A.   In many companies, management style is dependent on corporate culture and company philosophy. When that philosophy dictated a very strict interpretation of rules and procedures, I adhered to it. But there are many situations not covered by "the book," and in those situations my judgment was guided by the particular situation and the department's mission. My main goal is to get the work done, by people who perform their jobs with energy and initiative. It's very difficult to write how to do that into a policy manual.

Q.   Have you ever been in a position to delegate responsibility?

A.   Delegating responsibility is one of the first priorities of a manager. No matter how great or small my assignment, I developed a system for the work to go on even when I was not there. I prepare competent people to take my place successfully when I move on. This is one of the most difficult jobs a manager has, since it can interfere with his or her feeling of being indispensable. But only after you train someone to assume your duties are you ready to move up.

Q.   Have you ever been responsible for the profit and loss statements?

(If yes:)

A.   Yes, my position as _____ at _____ involved direct responsibility for the bottom line. I had the authority to make decisions that would affect the company P&Ls in the areas of _____, _____, and _____ . During the time I held that position, the company realized _____
(a XX percent increase in gross/net profit, or a similar statement. Choose and rehearse language that sounds objective and uses percentages.)

(If no, but if you do not want to rule out your potential skill in this area:)

I have never been directly responsible for the bottom line in the sense that management would come to me and ask me to explain why profits were not as projected or expected. However, my work has required me to keep an eye on methods that would produce efficiency and improve the overall financial picture of the company, and I have accomplished that with success. I would welcome both the responsibility for bottom line results and the authority to make decisions that would improve the P&L.

Q. How well do you manage people?

A.   I've experienced good results from the people management side of my work. I can communicate company goals and motivate people to produce. More than that, I've seen and tapped potential in my subordinates even they didn't realize existed. I'm pleased that (many/several) of those I initially trained and supervised eventually moved on to positions of greater responsibility in other departments and areas. This is a private legacy, and I'm proud of it.

34. Career objective questions: Make it clear what they hear.

Your "career objective" should vary depending on the target job. That's why I told you in *Jeff Allen's Best: The Resume* never to state your objective on your resume, and to be careful about what you write on an application form. Don't write the real one down either ("Getting this job"), even though that's what it is.

The jobsearch research you've been doing all along will help you customize this section of the script.

SCRIPT

Q. How important to you is the opportunity to reach the top?

A.   It's more a general goal than a constant ambition of mine. I know if I'm the best employee I can be, career advancement will take care of itself. Having a goal without hard work is like aiming at a target without ammunition. Working hard and enthusiastically is the best method for reaching the top.

I complete my work to the best of my ability and trust that, if I prove myself to be an asset to my employer, I'll be rewarded. So while the opportunity to reach the top is important to me, I know that opportunity only presents itself to those who earn it.

Q. Why do you want this job?

A. Because of the challenge, and the opportunities at _____ _____. I'm well qualified for it, and this is exactly the kind of _____ (competitive/creative/progressive/technically-oriented—use an appropriate adjective to the company and type of work) atmosphere I've been looking for. My career goal is _____ _____, and this job would allow me to develop my potential further while actively participating in that kind of work.

I've been offered a number of other opportunities; but after evaluating those jobs and companies, I decided not to make a move. Making a job change is a major decision, a long-term commitment that I take very seriously.

After researching the history and future plans of _____, meeting people who work here, and seeing the kinds of jobs there are to be done, it seems like a perfect fit!

Q. How long will you stay with the company?

A. As long as I continue to learn and develop my capabilities. As with any marriage, I intend to fulfill my commitment and meet challenges as they come.

It's my hope that as long as I perform well on the job and make contributions, I'll be considered a valuable employee. And as long as I'm making a contribution that is valued, I'll have no reason to leave. However, if for any reason I don't meet the company's expectations, I don't expect to remain on the payroll.

I've always approached a job as an important part of my life. There's a saying: "Work is not only the way to make a living; it's the way to make a life."

That says it all.

Q. What do you picture yourself doing (five/ten) years from now?

A. Five years from now, I see myself working for this company. My job will have increased at least one, probably two levels in responsibility and scope. I'll have made a significant contribution to the _____ department, and will be working on new ways to _____.

Ten years from now, I will have progressed up the ladder into general management. I'll have gotten there by proving I'm a producer, a problem solver, and someone who can grasp the scope of a program while not losing sight of the details.

Q. What are your long-term career objectives?

(Give specific details about the field or profession first, and what level you hope to attain within it.)

A. Essentially, I have given my career and opportunities a great deal of thought, and from that process I've developed a plan for achieving my long-term objective. This position is an important step in that long-term plan.

Q. Are your present career objectives different from your original goals?

A. Slightly. I made my plans at an early age. However, I modified them as I progressed and learned more about my capabilities and the work.

For a career plan to be useful—like any business plan—it must be flexible enough to respond to changes in the world of work. Career planning is an ongoing process, and several times throughout the years I have revised and updated my goals in response to new developments and opportunities.

Q. Would you consider a switch in careers at this point in your life?

A. Possibly. I'm very happy with my chosen field, have done well in it, and think there are things I can do even better as I progress upward.

However, I believe in being flexible and open to new opportunities. If you have a position in mind for me in the company that is different from work I've been doing, I'd like to explore it. I'm always interested in seeing how my background and skills can contribute to my success at a particular job.

Q. Would you be willing to relocate in the future?

(If the answer is an unqualified "yes":)

A. Definitely, yes. When I have moved or relocated in the past, new worlds of opportunity opened for me. Any major change, while always containing some risk, is a chance to grow, learn, and advance. All I need is a few days' notice, and I'll be ready.

(If the answer is a "qualified yes":)

Yes, if that relocation provided opportunity for advancement or for making a greater contribution to the company. My family is very supportive of my career. They know I would base such a decision on whether the move would be advantageous for them, too. I would evaluate the opportunity carefully; and if it was good, I'd need a little time to complete my commitments—both on the job and at home—before getting settled somewhere else.

(If you would rather not:)

My family and I have established our roots here. It's a great place to live, and we've made many friends in our community. Stability and continuity are important for raising a family.

I'd never reject a transfer without considering it seriously, however. I'd base my decision on whether the result would be a net gain—for the company, for my family, and for myself.

Q. Do you want to be president of this company?

A. Yes. I don't know too many capable, ambitious people who don't aspire to the highest management level within their companies. I aspire—but I perspire, too. It gets better results.

I also realize there are many other steps along the way where I can learn, contribute, and be rewarded in my work. I want to do the best job I can, moving on to the next challenge when I'm ready. If I continue to do that, I'll automatically rise to the top.

Q. When do you expect a promotion?

A. I would like my career to continue progressing as well as it has in the past. But I'm a realist. I know promotions aren't "given," they're earned. When I've mastered my present position, improved it with my ideas, prepared myself to take on new responsibilities, and trained someone to take over my job, I'll be ready for a promotion.

35. Questions about the target job: You suit it to a "t"!

If you've done your "phonework," it's just a matter of matching your background to the requirements and duties of the target job.

"Suitability" for a job is really just specialized use of certain learned information and practiced skills. Almost everything we do on the job (even a highly technical one) is common sense. Ask any supervisor and you'll find out how few employees specialize in that!

To match your skills to the target job and sell the interviewer on your suitability for it, do your job search research. Then, combine your unique background, experience, and qualifications with the interviewing skills you're learning here, and the job offers will follow. (Just don't flub your lines.)

SCRIPT

Q.   If we offer you a position and you accept it, how soon thereafter can you begin work?

A.   After giving my present employer two weeks' notice. As long as I know what's expected of me, there's no reason I can't plunge right into the new job. Procrastinating has a way of draining energy, which I could channel into my new job.

I have the enthusiasm and energy to get started. I'd also enjoy meeting the people I'll be working with so that we can develop a positive working relationship right away.

Some people like to take a vacation between jobs, but a vacation should be earned. I may have earned a vacation on my last job, but I intend to prove myself here at the earliest opportunity.

Q.   Would you be in a position to work overtime if required?

A.   Absolutely. A job is a lot more than a paycheck—it's a responsibility. I can understand that some people like to leave their work at the office and finish it the next day. But when I'm given a task to complete, I do so as soon as possible, even if it requires that I work overtime.

When I've been given the responsibility for a job, I take it seriously. I make sure what needs to get done, gets done. Whether I'm compensated for overtime or not, I derive personal satisfaction from the extra effort that results in success.

Extra effort makes the difference between a good job and a better one.

Q.   What do you know about our company?

(Do your jobsearch research, and single out two or three positive facts about the company, like growth in recent years, increasing market share, and innovative breakthroughs. Print these facts neatly on "cue cards"—3-by-5-inch index cards—for rehearsing your script. Just don't take your cue cards into the interview. You might also want to include any other information you picked up during your research, such as:)

A. Most important, I've heard that _____
(name of company) offers a challenging work environment that
expects a great deal from people and gives them the opportunity
to realize their potential. That's what I look for in an employer—
an active, creative environment where I am limited only by my
capability, and where positive results are acknowledged.

Q. What do you know about the position we have open?

(Again, demonstrate your initiative by offering a few facts about
the position you couldn't have learned from the advertisement.)

Q. Who do you think are our three major competitors?

A. I'd say _____ because
_____ ;
_____ ,
since_____; and probably
_____, because _____
_____
_____.

Q. Do they have any advantages over our company?

(While you want to show you are aware of competitors and their
products, be careful to balance any complimentary remarks
about them with equally complimentary remarks about the
employer. For example:)

A. I understand that _____ has a higher market
share in the _____ line, but _____'s
recent introduction of _____ is already being
received favorably and should surpass the competitive products
within the next 12 months.

(Or:)

_____ is well established, large, and has a higher
sales volume, but _____ has the advantage of
being more aggressive, innovative, and—it appears—more efficiently managed. You've already made impressive inroads into

their customer base. In the marketplace, _____ has the giants worried.

Q. What three trends do you see in the future for our industry?

(Take the time to prepare yourself for such a question, and be sure you can name three trends. Try to choose favorable ones. The following example would be suited to an employer in the communications industry.)

A.   First, as our economy has developed away from manufacturing and toward service jobs, the urgent need for better communication between people has become obvious. While the volume of paper increased steadily, communication—meaningful interaction—decreased.

Second, communication companies provide an indispensable service to people everywhere, helping them understand each other better. In the business environment, increased communication results in a better understanding among associates, employees, and customers. There's a definite trend toward more use of the services of companies such as _____ by all kinds of businesses to help them identify their needs and enhance their ability to meet them. There's a great potential for growth.

Third, the trend to desktop publishing should streamline operations in companies like this, decreasing cost and improving turnaround time to the customer. While some believe customers will invest in their own equipment and render our industry obsolete, there's little evidence this is happening. In fact, there's a trend toward increased use of outside service companies like _____, to avoid the high cost of full-time employees.

All in all, the future looks very bright for this industry. That's why I'm here.

Q. What interests you about our company?

A.   I've been very impressed in all the reading and research I've done about _____. It projects an excellent image, and its message is persuasive. Internally, it's a sound operation, with ambitious goals and realistic plans for achieving them.

I see great potential for growth here, and I want to be part of it. I have many ideas that I know could be implemented here better than anywhere else.

Q. What single thing about our product or service interests you most?

(As before, you must be prepared for this one. Know something about the company and what it does, such as:)

A. I understand your computer systems have the least maintenance downtime of any on the market. For an account executive, that's an important sales advantage. You're offering them more value and efficiency for their investment.

(Or:)

You just introduced an innovative life insurance package, and you're the only company in the industry that offers benefit flexibility like that. I'd like to be able to work with a creative organization whose products offer its customers the "leading edge" in life insurance protection.

Q. Why would you be happy doing this type of work?

A. Because it's the kind of work I've always enjoyed doing. All the tests I took early in my career said I was best suited for this kind of work. I agreed, and made my career plans accordingly.

Someone who likes his or her work demonstrates enthusiasm, initiative, and energy that others can't match. There's a great law of life that few people realize: We like most what we do best, and we do best what we like most!

Q. What specific ways will our company benefit from hiring you?

A. It will be getting someone whose skills and training most closely match the job requirements. Further, it will be getting the

benefit of my experience at _____,
_____, and _____.

My background relates directly to the position being considered and is a primary reason why it will take me less time to produce than someone who hasn't had as much direct experience.

Further, I'm dedicated and learn quickly. I try always to excel at what I do; so, when you hire me, there's little risk you'll be interviewing for the job again soon.

Q. What do you believe are your special qualifications for this job?

(Begin by mentioning any specific training and experience that apply to the position. Then:)

A. As a result of my background, I have direct insight into the requirements of this job and know how to increase _____
_____ (efficiency/productivity/sales).

Further, I'm driven to achieve, to surpass my most recent record, so you'll never see me turn in a merely "acceptable" performance. I really think from all you've told me that the position could use someone with my attributes. There are a great many challenges to be met, and the right person—someone who approaches them with energy and determination—will achieve results greater than anyone thought possible. I believe I'm that right person.

Q. How do you manage to interview while still employed?

A. I'm using personal time I've earned, since I rarely take sick leave. I manage my interview schedule, and I try not to be away from my job more than one day at a time.

Sometimes it means working extra hours, but I take my responsibilities seriously. No one has to cover for me. In addition, I check in through the day for messages and to see if any situations need attention.

I've developed a system for the work flow. As a result, no order sits on my desk, and nothing is delayed in my absence.

Employees do themselves and their employers a disservice by getting themselves overloaded or in a position where they are the only ones who can do a job. If you take care of the little things, the big ones take care of themselves. A little organization, self-discipline, and prioritizing go a long way.

Q. Do you feel you are ready for a more responsible position? Tell me why you think so.

A. Yes, definitely. When you cease to be challenged, you stop growing. I've gone as far as I can go in my present job. My manager is very pleased with my work, but the _____ (size of the company/present economic environment) limits additional responsibility in the foreseeable future.

    I know I am capable of greater achievements, which is why I'm interviewing for this position. There's a challenge offered here that I'm ready to meet.

Q. Is there one particular trait or skill you possess that should lead us to consider you above other candidates?

(Think about your answer to this question in terms of your particular abilities and how they apply to the target job. Then tell and sell.

    Are you a fast typist or programmer? If the job is customer-service or otherwise people-oriented, do you have the ability to make others respond favorably? In the lines provided, formulate the first part of your answer, being sure to mention what you think is the most prominent of your own unique and proven skills. Then follow up with the scripted paragraph following.)

A. _____
_____
_____
_____
_____

    In addition to that, I have the drive to take on this job and do it well. In fact, I think I'll excel at it.

Q. May we contact your present employer?

(If your employer does not know you are interviewing, smile—don't giggle—and say:)

A. No. I haven't told my employer. So please let me know before you contact anyone there. Once there's a firm offer on the table, or you've narrowed the field to only a few candidates, the information I've given you can be verified.

My boss deserves the courtesy of hearing I'm leaving from me. (He'll/She'll) be upset, but I'll assure (him/her) everything will be done to ensure the most efficient transfer of my duties. You'll probably get more than a reference—you might get a testimonial!

(If your employer knows you are interviewing and would give you a good reference:)

Yes, my employer knows I am interviewing, and understands the reason. We've had a good working relationship for the past ___ years. But now I've reached the highest level possible there, and I've trained people to assume my duties.

My boss regrets not being able to offer me more at this time, and understands that I'm not working to my full potential. We're parting on good terms. (He/She) even told me recently, "That's the price you sometimes pay for hiring and training the best people." All of what I've told you will be confirmed when you call. But please let me know first, so I can let (him/her) down gently.

Q. Aren't you overqualified for this job?

A. Although I already know the job we're discussing, my background will enable me to eventually expand it into something more. I may be more qualified than others you're considering, but every job can be enhanced by being creative.

With my qualifications, I can do the job right away. Then, the company will benefit from my additional experience, and I'll be able to do more with the position than has been done in the past. In that way, I'll continue to be challenged—and you'll be acquiring someone with additional potential.

I've learned many techniques for improving the efficiency and productivity of this type of operation. I'd welcome the opportunity to use what I know to improve things here.

So, while I might be starting out at a slightly lower level of responsibility, this company is growing and going places. I see a lot of opportunity here.

36. Questions about salary history and requirements: Get more!

Salary "history" and "requirements" are really two separate issues. Salary history should be (but isn't) illegal to ask. What does some other employer's idea of your value have to do with *this* employer's? Even if it had some marginal significance, benefits and job duties are never the same.

Salary questions are asked because they're a perfect way to tell you you're "overqualified" or "just not senior enough." They screen you out in the safest way, without risking a visit from the equal employment authorities.

Most of the time, you'll be earning less in your current job than the target job pays, so give yourself every chance to increase current salary. Will you be receiving an increase soon? Do you get supercharged overtime? Is there an automatic bonus system? Pay in lieu of vacation? You won't be taking a vacation if you accept a new job. When benefits and nonsalary compensation are added up, most jobs "pay" 20 to 30 percent more than people write on applications. Doesn't your boss remind you of this from time to time? Remind your boss of that fact when the time comes to confirm your salary.

As with everything else, be honest. But be fair to yourself. They shouldn't be asking the question in the first place.

Salary requirements are a trap just waiting to be sprung. The chances of your being too high or too low on a resume or application are almost 1 to 1. Your real salary requirement is "more," but if you must answer the question in that little rectangle or line on the application, write "Open." If it says, "Don't write 'Open'," write "Negotiable." Spell it correctly, though.

Keep your options open until you're in the interview, where you can drive up your value and safely state just the right amount. I don't know of a single case over the past 25 years where an employer has rejected someone before an interview for not stating a specific salary requirement on a resume or application. But I know of hundreds of applicants whose salary numbers excluded them.

Applicants are concerned with eating, so they don't realize how negotiable and unimportant salary is to employers. Even the most structured compensation systems allow for hiring above the "rate range." Creating additional positions for the exceptions is done all the time.

Artificial salary constraints are a great negotiating tool, but they rarely stop employers from getting someone they want. Don't let them stop you. Instead, carefully plan your answers to the inevitable questions. Here's how:

SCRIPT

Q. What salary are you worth?

A. An employee's worth is measured by his or her contribution to an employer. I expect to contribute and to be paid a salary commensurate with that contribution. I know you'll be fair—otherwise I wouldn't accept or stay.

Once hired, my first priority is to do the job I'm being paid to do. And, if I perform well, I expect to advance accordingly. However, money is not foremost in my mind. Too much concern about the paycheck can lead to a poor attitude and result in a poor job. As long as my focus is doing the best job possible, I doubt I'll have anything to worry about.

Q. Do you expect to be rewarded for work you consider to be well done?

A. Not necessarily. In the world of work, the rewards don't always follow the effort.

Like most people, I want to have my income increase. But,

as a mature person, I realize that there are other considerations, too. Recognition in the form of monetary reward is always gratifying, but it can be more fulfilling to meet a challenge with success, and see the results of your efforts on the job. That's a personal type of reward no amount of money can buy.

I've always looked upon making a living as only one part of making a life. The feeling I get when my extra effort results in excellence is the real reward. If others don't recognize my achievements, there's always the next project.

Q. What would you like to be earning (two/five/ten) years from now?

A. At any point in my career, I'd like my salary to keep pace with inflation and be competitive with what similar positions pay.

However, I don't see myself as an "average" employee. I always strive for "excellent" and never settle for anything less than "above average." So, logically, my income should reflect that.

As long as my paycheck is an investment by the company that earns a return, the higher the rate of return the more it should invest. If I'm not performing at any time, I shouldn't be here. I have no illusions about employment as a value-for-value relationship.

Q. What is your salary history?

A. I'd be happy to give you specific numbers, and percentages of increase, from year to year, but I'm not able to recite them from memory now. Salary just isn't as important to me as opportunity.

At every salary review, I received merit increases. My salary has always been a reflection of my work progress and contribution to my employer's success. Anything less than that doesn't work for long.

Q. Have you ever been turned down for a salary increase?

A. I haven't had to "ask" for a "raise." My performance evaluations were always positive, and my salary reviews consistently resulted in increases. In some years, the increases were lower than in others due to overall financial conditions. But, have I ever been refused a raise because of inadequate performance? No.

Q.   Do you have any outside income?

(This is none of their business and shouldn't even be considered when determining your suitability for the job. Your spouse's income is not yours, so your answer should be "no." They don't need to know that you receive a nice monthly check from a trust fund set up by a grandparent. "Child support payments" are income you receive on behalf of your children, not yourself. So, unless you have another job or income from a business on the side, your answer is always "no."

Of course, if you're in the National Guard or any of the military reserves, do explain. Since most employers support these, consenting to a little invasion of privacy might advance you directly from maneuvers onto the battlefield.

But, if you do derive additional income from part-time or self-employment, plan your response thoughtfully. Will the interviewer perceive your "moonlighting" as an interference with the target job? Consider this sample answer:)

I occasionally work part time in the evenings or on weekends as a (bartender/private duty nurse/CIA operative) but I have no other professional commitment on a regular basis. I have the right of refusal, and the people I work with understand my priorities. I never let "fill-in" work interfere with my primary job. It's just been a source of extra income from time to time.

Q.   How far can you lower your salary expectations to be in line with our rate for the position?

A.   It would be difficult to accept much less than my present salary. I don't know too many people who want to lower their standard of living.

However, if you can tell me when my salary would increase and to what level, based on my satisfactory progress, I would consider a temporary cut.

Q. What is your current salary?

(Sit down with a pencil and paper now, and add up the worth of pay in lieu of vacation, profit-sharing, bonuses, pension plans, stock purchase plans, and the other "not-very fringes." Don't forget the value of a company car, tuition reimbursement, and even subsidized meals in the cafeteria. If you're currently paying 2 dollars a day for a hot lunch, that's about 30 dollars less a week than you'd have to spend on the outside. And don't forget to add 20 percent for the tip.

Estimates of the dollar value of "perks" range as high as 30 percent of salary. Some companies send an annual statement telling you the dollar value of the benefits you receive. Use it in determining your answer.)

My base salary is _____ ($48,000). With overtime, end-of-year bonus, company-matched savings plans, pension and profit sharing, I earn _____ ($60,000) excluding complete medical insurance coverage.

---

37. Experience and training questions: You've got the experience express card!

Experience isn't what you've done; it's what you *do* with what you've done. Everyone who is the same age has the same amount of experience—it's just that each person has it in different areas. Those different areas are really just matters of *focus*.

When you prepared your super-resume according to the tips in *Jeff Allen's Best: The Resume,* you took an experience inventory. Review those notes now to prepare this section of your script.

SCRIPT

Q. How did you get into the type of work you are doing now?

(The first part of your answer should include specific information about the career path that led you to your present job. Scratch out your script in the lines provided. Then close with the paragraph following:)

_____

_____

_____

_____

_____

_____

_____

_____

Considering my educational background, my interest in _____, and the satisfaction I derive from completing a job properly, I decided to become a _____.

I don't think I'd be able to really excel if I weren't truly interested in the job, or if I were merely motivated by its financial rewards. However, since I find the work both challenging and fulfilling, the better I do the more I enjoy it.

Q. Why are you leaving your present position?

A.   I need to be challenged to develop my potential further. I'm interested in additional responsibility and new opportunity, which unfortunately are limited at _____ (name of current employer) because of _____ (company size/limited product line/restructuring or downsizing).

The reputation and market focus of _____ _____ (name of prospective employer) offer many opportunities for someone with my training and experience. It's the optimum kind of environment I've been seeking.

Q.   How would you compare the quality of your work to that of others in the same job?

A.   The quality of my work has been consistently as good as— or better than—my coworkers'. I've always met or exceeded expectations.

Some people pay too much attention to the work that others around them are doing. If they're doing more, they lower their speed to the average. I'm just not that kind of person. I set my pace according to what is required by the job, and I always try to beat the clock and my own record.

People spend more time on the job than anywhere else. I owe it to myself and my employer to make every minute count. If I just kept doing the average work, at an average pace, life would be awfully boring. So I don't wait for challenges to be dropped in my lap. I go out and find them!

Q. What factors contribute the most to your success on your present job?

A. First, experience. The training and situations in my previous jobs helped me go further and faster on this job. My jobs have increased in responsibility, with each level building on the last.

Second, continuing education. In addition to formal schooling, I've always taken the time to be informed and current on what I needed to know to be effective. I attend seminars and workshops, take courses, and I always have professional or management materials available to read when I'm waiting somewhere.

Which leads me to the third reason for my success: good planning and productive use of time. When I run into roadblocks on the job, I figure out a way to eliminate them or at least turn them into speed bumps.

Wasting time while you're waiting for something to happen drains energy. If Plan A is temporarily on hold, I immediately swing into Plans B, C, D, and so on. It's amazing how much nonproductive time can be turned into job improvement if you're just aware of how to do it.

Q. What specific strengths do you think you can bring to this position?

(Sample answer:)

A. My education in _____, my experience in

_____, and my knowledge in the area of
_____ all will contribute to my performing this
position with little or no "downtime." I have the proven ability
to transfer my skills from one job to another.

Because of this, I can learn my way around an organization
quickly. I can concentrate on motivating and managing the staff
quickly while developing relationships with other supervisors.

**Q. Can you explain the long gaps in your employment
history?**

(This is a tough one. If there are long gaps, your answer should
offer a brief, believable explanation, and then you should convince the interviewer why this won't affect your ability to
succeed at the target job.)

A. When I was younger, the decisions I made seemed right at
the time. Although these choices don't appear on my resume, I
learned a lot along the way.

In one case, I believed I needed more education and training
to achieve my goals, so I left work and re-enrolled in college. That
decision was justified, because when I returned to the work force
it was at a higher level of responsibility and pay. Not only did I
learn critical skills, I learned the self-discipline formal study
requires.

Another time I had the opportunity to serve on board a three-
masted schooner on an expedition in the South Seas. While being
a deck hand didn't add to my computer programming knowledge,
I learned the value of hard work, team effort, and overcoming
hardship. Everyone should learn those values. It really helps to
supercharge a career.

I've had life experiences I can bring to bear on the job. My
track record for the past _____ years has been consistent
and progressive, and my work has increased in responsibility.

I have set my career goals and developed a plan for achieving
them. That, combined with my family responsibilities, make me
a very stable employee and a good risk.

(Now, your answer:)

Q.   In what areas have you received compliments from your supervisors?

A.   I have always had high marks in job effectiveness, initiative, and enthusiasm. Because I look at each assignment as a potentially exciting challenge, my managers say I create excitement in my department. That spirit is contagious. It results in greater team effort, less absenteeism, and higher output.

38.   "Outside interest" questions can get you *inside*!

If you were applying at a dating service, this would be an important area. Otherwise, your outside interests don't affect your ability to do your job. However, for the time being, you do have an important *inside* interest: delivering your script and successfully passing this part of the screen test.

If the company is really big on charity drives, mention your assistance to charities. If it encourages employees to participate in civic activities, mention that. Most people have enough outside interests they can convert to "inside" interests as soon as the curtain rises.

How do successful interviewees learn how to answer these questions? Through keen powers of observation. Before they ever enter the interviewer's office, they've "scoped out" the company's offices and made mental notes of trophies, awards, citations, photos, and any other physical clues that reveal what is important to the company. Earlier phone sleuthing might have revealed information about company trips, picnics, and blood drives as well.

I was a personnel manager for a company that wouldn't hire anyone who didn't lift weights. Was it discriminatory? Yes. Was it unfair? Yes. Was it ridiculous? Yes. Was it legal? Yes.

Did I liberalize the definition of "lifting weights" for otherwise qualified applicants? Yes.

SCRIPT

Q. How interested are you in sports?

A. I like playing them more than watching them. Some require mental discipline. Some require a cooperative team effort. But all reward those who are the best.

Sports are sometimes violent and unproductive, but they can also teach valuable lessons. If someone doesn't have much self-esteem, sports can help him or her develop into a high achiever. The message is that hard work can pay off. In sports, people learn their limitations, too. No one can be best at everything. Learning your weaknesses can help you develop your strengths.

Q. What are your leisure-time activities?

(Before answering this question, conduct a split-second mental review of the clues you picked up on your way in. If this company appears "activity-oriented," and you play racquetball but also collect stamps, emphasize racquetball. If you know something about the company culture—an emphasis on family values, for example—concentrate on that aspect of your life.)

A. My dedication to my career takes up most of my time. However, I make it a point every day to spend time with my family. I'm involved in my kids' sports and help them with their homework. After that, I settle down and catch up on my work-related reading—journals and other trade publications.

Weekends are spent in family activities, gardening, social events, and community affairs.

(Now your answer:)

_____

_____

_____

_____

_____

Q.   What were your extracurricular activities in school?

(If the target job requires leadership skills, accent your leadership activities. If physical stamina and conditioning are required, mention your sports achievements. If it is a people-oriented occupation, tell about community involvement.)

A.   I was captain of the debating team and vice-president of the senior class. My extracurricular activities in school served to guide me in my career choices. Leadership roles, where effective communication is required, come naturally to me.

(Or:)

My extracurricular activities in high school and college centered around sports—mainly football and track. Being active and staying in top physical condition are still important to me, since they make me more effective in everything I do.

(Now your answer:)

_____

_____

_____

_____

_____

Q.   What is your favorite television program?

(Just try answering *Wheel of Fortune* or *I Love Lucy* reruns and see how fast the spotlights go out and the curtain falls. Answer

Masterpiece Theater and you might be labeled "too highbrow." Try to chart a middle course.)

A.   There isn't much time in my life for watching television other than the evening news. Occasionally, I see if there's something interesting to watch. I like business-oriented specials and news features the best.

Q.   Have you ever been the head of a committee?

(This is a good chance to mention community leadership and organization experience. Even if you haven't participated in recent years, see if you can find something to score a few extra points.)

Yes, several times. Most recently, I chaired the annual fund raising event for _____, a local service club. I've headed up several different committees for that organization in past years.

I had a great deal of leadership experience as a teenager as well. I was actively involved in youth fund-raising efforts for the March of Dimes and other causes, often taking a leadership role.

Citizenship means more than paying taxes and keeping your yard clean. I try to get involved and assist whenever I can.

Q.   Do you consider yourself a social drinker?

(A moderate answer is your best bet here. You have no way of knowing, but the company may prohibit any alcohol use by employees during working hours. Or you may be in the midst of a real "office party" culture where nondrinkers are ostracized.)

I enjoy an occasional glass of wine with a formal dinner. But I can take or leave alcohol in social situations. At business functions where clients are present, I tend to have at most one drink to be sure I stay alert and represent the company to the best of my ability.

Q.   Does your social life include associates and coworkers?

From time to time it has. I have many outside interests, however, and many friends that I know through them.

I enjoy company functions, but my social life doesn't revolve around work. I prefer to strike a good balance between my personal and professional activities. It's easier to handle difficult situations with coworkers when they aren't good friends.

This "professional detachment" doesn't mean you can't be sensitive to the needs of others. It just makes the relationship more objective and businesslike. We're being paid to do a job—there's really not much time for socializing when we're doing it.

Q. What are you doing to improve yourself?

A. Self-improvement should be part of everyone's life. I educate myself informally through reading. I try to learn something new on a regular basis by reading an article on an unfamiliar topic. I also review self-help techniques in books and magazines. It keeps me sharp.

(If applicable:)

I'm presently taking a course in _____ at
_____, as well.

Beyond that, I maintain optimum health through regular exercise and proper diet, and I follow a routine of _____
_____ .

39. Your turn: Questions to ask the interviewer.

Although they don't require great acting ability to deliver, questions you ask the interviewer demonstrate your interest in the job. *And* they give you the opportunity to lead the interviewer into your strongest areas.

Your questions and the interviewer's answers shouldn't exceed 10 percent of the total interview time. Since you don't know how long the interview will last, just ask a question after you have answered around nine of them. Don't sit there writing tally marks on your resume—just keep track mentally. If you ask two questions in a row, wait a little longer before you ask about something else.

Asking questions is an important part of "pacing" and "leading" the interview. These techniques are covered in the next section. Questioning must be done naturally, at optimum times and in a nonthreatening manner. No question should be asked unless you are certain the answer will make you appear *interested*, *intelligent*, and *qualified*.

Proper questioning helps you align your answers to the areas the interviewer considers significant. It also gives you feedback to check your alignment.

Listen for company and industry buzzwords to use as the interview progresses. Above all, don't interrupt or argue with the interviewer.

The average applicant talks about 85 percent of the time during an interview. That's why average applicants don't get hired. They're amateur solo acts with monotonous monologues who nervously bang their gums on the interviewer's drums. Then, both of them march out the door together and only the interviewer returns.

Applicants who get hired zip the lip 50 percent of the time. This is one of the most accurate indicators of whether an offer will be extended—and *you* can control it.

Use questions as zippers to help you. Don't ask personal, controversial, or negative questions of any kind. Stay away from asking anything that will lead into sensitive areas. Invariably, salary and benefits should be avoided—I've shown you how to answer the interviewer's questions about them properly.

Here are examples of benign questions that have a favorable impact:

SCRIPT

1. How many employees does the company have?
2. What are the company's plans for expansion?
3. How many employees does the department have?
4. Is the department a profit center?
5. Does the department work separately from other departments?

6. Are the functions of the department important to senior management?

7. Is the relationship between the department and senior management favorable?

8. What is the supervisor's management style?

9. What is the supervisor's title?

10. Who does the supervisor report to?

11. Are you ready and able to hire now?

12. How long will it take to make a hiring decision?

13. How long has the position been open?

14. How many employees have held the position in the past five years?

15. Why are the former employees no longer in the position?

16. How many employees have been promoted from the position in the past five years?

17. What does the company consider the five most important duties of the position?

18. What do you expect the employee you hire to accomplish?

Take One and Roll 'Em

With your script rehearsed and your lines learned, you're ready for the "director's" screen test. Some final acting lessons and stage direction follow in the next chapter.

Chapter

3

The Screen Test: Your Interview

By now, you're researched, rehearsed, and re-dressed. Ready to deliver the performance of your livelihood. That's how you have to approach each interview. As if your career depended on it. It does.

Once inside, the following techniques help you stay in the spotlight, and away from the tomatoes. When the standing ovation stops, you'll need to know which offer to accept. N-i-i-i-ce.

40. Make the first impression the best.

In the first few minutes, interviewers either choose or snooze. Some don't even take that long. Like movie critics (and every other decision maker), they remain only to justify their judgment. Often, it's merely to get more ammunition for a critical blasting.

Your critics are beyond busy. They're diverted, distracted, and disarranged. They discuss, disapprove, and dismiss so many hopefuls that first impressions become *only* ones. Yes—they discriminate disproportionately, disobeying the law. It's not intentional, but neither is any survival instinct.

You can do far more to help them than an army of affirmative action officers. Stereotyping, like insisting on resumes, is a matter of survival. Just be sure you're "stereotypecast" in the role known as the target job.

If the pressure is hard to believe, consider that, in companies with fewer than 500 employees, it is not unusual for wage and salary, insurance, employee benefits, labor relations, affirmative action, management development, security, medical, training, safety, mail, telephone operations, plant maintenance, food service, company functions, civic activities, and a variety of other administrative duties to be performed by the individual who just escorted you into the office to talk about the same position as all those other clamoring candidates in the lobby.

Your first number must be a showstopper. That's why I recommend you:

41. Use the "magic four hello."

This initial, programmed, perfect greeting consists of the following four components:

1. A smile. (Genuine. Not just with the mouth, but the eyes as well. Practice.)
2. Direct eye contact. (Straightforward, self-assured, friendly.)
3. The words, "Hi, I'm (first name) (last name). It's a pleasure meeting you."
4. A firm handshake. (No live sharks; no dead flounders.)

The "magic four" are simple enough on the surface, but it takes practice to perfect these four elements and convey a natural ease and confidence to your interviewer. You probably think you do everything right. It's unlikely, though. Only 10 percent of all jobseekers are in that category.

42. Hone your handshake.

Aside from making the "magic four" flow naturally, a proper handshake is often the hardest technique to master.

The negative impression that a hapless handshake leaves behind can completely obstruct the rest of your interview performance. It's as if the curtain never goes up, the lights never go on, and the audience is lined up at the popcorn stand.

The handshake sets the tempo of the interview. If you have either of the problems mentioned previously—a shark that sprains or a flounder that flops—practice shaking hands with your other hand. You may look funny, but you'll get hired. (You might get to know yourself better, too!)

In *Contact: The First Four Minutes*, Leonard Zunin emphasized the importance of first impressions. He devoted an *entire chapter* to the handshake. Here's what he wrote:

> A moist palm may merely show someone is nervous, a symbol which automatically eliminates any job applicant at at least one large company of which I am aware. Its personnel director once told me that regardless of the qualifications of a man he interviews, "if his handshake is weak and clammy, he's out." Such reaction to body language is far more prevalent than we realize, as others assume many things about our glance, stance, or advance.
>
> We shake hands thousands of times in a lifetime, and it is unfortunate that most of us get little or no feedback on whether or not others like or dislike our handshake.[4]

43. Don't address the interviewer by his or her first name.

Not in any telephone or mail contact or during the interview itself unless the interviewer requests that you do. It should always be "Mr." or "Ms." If the interviewer addresses you by your first name, ask if you may reciprocate: "Mr. Carlson—may I call you John?"

44. Avoid assuming a subordinate role.

It's only natural to go slow in a new situation. Fear of the unknown, dependence on circumstances beyond your control, and being under close scrutiny can cause you to play a subordinate role.

But this is no time to hide in the wings. Crawling doesn't work, either. It's the time to put your best foot forward. The rest of your body generally follows.

Here are techniques to maintain emotional balance, size up the situation, and give an "A" audition.

45. Admire something in the interviewer's office.

When you enter the office, admire something like a company award, a desk accessory, or an item of furniture. Stay away from family pictures, clothing, and other personal items. It's too soon. By admiring the right thing, you're buying some time to:

46. Assess the interviewer's style.

This is essential. In those first few moments, while greetings are exchanged and seats are taken, you must be alert for clues to the interviewer's personality. If you can determine his or her style, and adjust yours to be compatible, you're getting hired. You'll be able to communicate successfully and develop rapport with the interviewer. No credentials or experience are as powerful as this.

Communication authorities categorize personalities according to specific traits. If you "read" certain clues given by the individual and his or her environment, you can decide how to proceed.

47. Recognize the four basic personality types.

Most authorities divide people into four personality types:

Type 1: Outgoing and Direct

This person is called the "socializer." He or she is energetic, friendly, and self-assured.

Ways to spot this personality include:

1. A flamboyant style of dress. Even in a conservative business suit, a brightly colored tie or scarf might be worn. He or she prefers current fashion to classic styles.

2. Many pictures and personal mementos in the office.

3. A cluttered desk, or at least a covered one.

4. Little time-consciousness so could keep you waiting. In most cases, he or she is juggling a hundred things at once.

These types gravitate toward personnel jobs because they're outgoing "people people."

If you're a methodical, reserved type, you can get into trouble with this kind of interviewer. You'll have to smile more, talk faster, and get to the point. They have to *like* you before they'll listen to you. And listening is not on their list.

If you're this type, be careful. You don't want to outtalk, outsmile, or outinterview the interviewer.

Besides, lunging across the desk might frighten him or her away.

Type 2: Self-Contained and Direct

This type is referred to as the "director." "Dictator" is more descriptive, though. They differ from socializers because they're far more reserved and conservative. Before unconventional computer kids started running companies, it was believed you had to be like this to make top management. They're still among the high achievers in every field.

Clues to this personality are:

1. A conservative, quality, custom-tailored wardrobe—impeccably worn.

2. A neat, organized work space. A few expensive personal desk accessories. Perhaps one or two classic picture frames containing family photos. Nothing flashy. Understated.

3. A firm handshake, but not much of a smile. Not as talkative as the first type. They'll size *you* up—critically—and wait for you to make your mistakes.

4. Someone who's time conscious and annoyed when others are not. Goal- and bottom-line oriented. Believes that all work and no play is the way to spend the day.

To get along with this type, be all business. Don't waste his or her time. Eliminate unnecessary words and be sincere. This type itches around "touchy-feely" people. You won't find this interviewer saying, "Oh, I just *adore* this." You shouldn't, either.

Don't let him or her intimidate you, either. If you do, he or she will sense it and reject you immediately. Don't be defensive about weaknesses in your background. Just explain them by turning them into strengths.

Type 3: Self-Contained and Indirect

They're called "thinkers" and might be found in analytical professions. They don't speak up, socialize, or editorialize. They go about their work quietly, and they get it done properly.

Evidence of this personality includes:

1. Uninteresting, understated clothes. Gray and beige predominate. Style and looks aren't a priority. Function is. This person is nothing if not practical.

2. Few personal items and "warm fuzzies."

3. Unless he or she has been looking for a job and reading this book, this type's hand will probably dangle at the end of his or her wrist. Shake it anyway—it will confirm your suspicions that he or she is a "thinker."

4. Time conscious and work oriented. The thinker's work ethic is just as strong as the director's, but he or she doesn't want to run things. He or she is a loner.

5. An organized desk, with neatly arranged work. Maybe even a "To Do" list with half the items crossed off.

This person is hard to draw out, and may become annoyed if you try. If you're pushy and aggressive, he or she will withdraw and your offer will be withheld. Answer questions directly and succinctly, and volunteer as much information as he or she needs to make a decision. This interviewer thrives on data, but needs time to analyze it. So don't rush.

Type 4: Outgoing and Indirect

The most common word for them is "helpers." They're friendly like socializers, but without the aggressiveness. Helpers tend to gravitate toward "human resources"—they're the closest business gets to providing psychiatric social work for employees.

Helpers take time to know you before the actual interview begins. They're "nice," but will do almost anything to avoid making a decision. In that area, *you* need to help *them*. You're probably talking to a helper when there is:

1. A nonthreatening appearance that matches the interviewer's demeanor. Neutral shades, soft fabrics.
2. A number of personal items on his or her desk—often handmade. The office will reflect that other people are important to him or her.
3. A friendly, expressive, and concerned approach. This type may apologize for keeping you waiting because he or she was busy solving everyone else's problems. He or she will smile warmly, reach out to take your hand, and might never let it go.
4. A phone ringing, work piling up, and many uncompleted projects. To this interviewer, "people" are all that matter.

This person is the opposite of the "director" type, and they rarely play opposite each other. Certainly not in love scenes. That's why CEOs tend to be on the top floor while personnel is in the basement. The helper never gives up trying to convince the director to "humanize," "personalize," and "realize."

To get hired, take time to establish rapport, become friends,

and accentuate the importance of the "person" in "personnel."
But remember to limit interviews to forty-five minutes.

With a helper, it's *your* responsibility to get your job qualifications across. If you don't, you may leave the interview with
a friend but not a job. The interviewer won't ask you to give him
or her a reason to hire you or even recommend you for a second
interview.

Emotionally, he or she doesn't realize that's why you're
there. He or she thinks it's because you're taking a hiring survey.
This type helps, but doesn't hire.

This is a remarkably accurate way to out-stereotype the
stereotypers. Some will fit the description exactly, others will fit
several. No matter—just know and play to your audience. Study
the four profiles and practice typecasting a few of your friends, coworkers, and relatives. Learn to pick up on the clues to someone's
predominant personality style. Then practice playing to them.
They're your audience, too!

Picking up clues from a person's appearance, speech, and
body language can serve you in many ways throughout your
career. Use this little system well!

---

48. Align with the interviewer.

Will Rogers said, "I never met a man I didn't like."

Jeff Allen says, "Neither did I. That's why I never saw a job
I couldn't get."

Do you know people who seem to have the knack for getting
any job they want, when they want it? Do you wish you knew
their "secret"? There's no secret. They simply learned that *liking*
the interviewer has a dramatic, positive effect. It invokes a powerful rule of human motivation: PEOPLE LIKE PEOPLE WHO
LIKE THEM.

In *Power! How to Get It, How to Use It*, Michael Korda said:

A great deal can be gained by simply learning to smile, an
exercise which is not all that easy for many people to perform.
The person who wants to use power must learn to control his
facial muscles, his temper and himself, and avoid taking

"tough stands" where they aren't necessary. Flexibility and cheerfulness are better weapons than brute force, and if used properly have the advantage of making your rivals forget that you're a competitor for power.[5]

An employment interview is a place to be *liked*. Unless you're likeable, you won't be hireable.

On my first day as an employment interviewer, I was warned to avoid the "halo effect." Twenty-five years later, I still can't tell you how to do this. The halo effect is a phenomenon that occurs when the interviewer identifies with the candidate. Once it happens, he or she can't do or say anything wrong. He or she is hopelessly hired. The halo effect gives you a psychological advantage that will zap any interviewer into submission within seconds.

As I wrote in *How to Turn an Interview into a Job*:

The formula for your ammunition is carefully secreted within the July 1979 issue of *Psychology Today*. If you want to learn its detailed ingredients, go directly to your local public library, find it, and turn to page 66. There it is: "People Who Read People," by Daniel Goleman. The ammunition is known as "pacing."

Pacing is an accepted psychological technique which has been developed to increase rapport with others. It stems from an even more powerful law of human motivation: WE LIKE PEOPLE WHO ARE LIKE OURSELVES. If you think about it, our entire hiring process is guided by this law. So is almost every other human decision we make about others, including voting, selection of spouses and friends, television and radio choices, product purchases, etc. For our highly specialized purpose, it means *aligning* yourself with the overworked and underpaid interviewer, and then leading (steering) him almost imperceptibly, but irresistibly, into extending the offer.

I use pacing all the time in court proceedings, administrative hearings, negotiations, and other difficult situations. You can win the ones you thought were lost if you know how to do it properly. I introduced the concept of pacing to placement services in my seminars. . . . It has been so effective in influencing hiring authorities, that many of them have incorporated the techniques . . . in their standard operating procedures. It even works over the telephone. . . . You simply must have a common ground before you can move toward a mutual goal.[6]

The next seven items are a step-by-step guide for developing your own skill at pacing.

49. Attempt to sit next to the interviewer.

If there's a couch in the office, stand there until you are asked to be seated, since that's the best place for your interview. You create an atmosphere of "you and me against the job requisition" rather than "you against me."

The opportunity will probably arise to sit on your favored side (your right—the interviewer's left—if you're right-handed, etc.). This is because over 95 percent of the time there are two chairs facing the interviewer. That favored side is psychologically your *power* side. Sitting there will help you interview more confidently.

Look for an opportunity to walk around to the interviewer's side during the interview so you can look at some report, chart, or project "together."

Remember the lessons of the four personality types. The director and thinker personalities need more space between themselves and you. They're not comfortable with air space invasions and could react negatively if you move in too close.

50. "Mirror" the interviewer's body language, facial expressions, eye movement, rate of speech, tone of voice, and rate of breathing.

Note that I said "mirror," not "mimic." This is a subtle art, and you'll need practice to get it right. However, the results will amaze and amuse you. This subtle form of imitation is a proven way to establish rapport. Just be careful to *align*, not *offend*. With practice, mirroring will become natural for you—it's a basic form of physical agreement.

51. Use "insider" language.

The company buzzwords and insider language I told you to leave off your resume in *Jeff Allen's Best: The Resume* should be used during the interview. Every group has its own verbal shorthand that its members use constantly.

The primary use of insider language in pacing is to lock in the alignment with the interviewer. It's a linguistic password that gets you into his or her thinking process and allows you to lead. It also signifies you're compatible with the corporate culture.

"Company" buzzwords should be heard and noted in your jobsearch research and phonework. Understand and use them correctly.

As for the "employment" buzzwords (near and dear to any human resourcer's heart), here's all you need to know from *How to Turn an Interview into a Job*:

Acceptance. The easiest response to any job offer. "When do I start?" are the words used.

Available labor pool. What you are walking on, rather than swimming in.

Contact information. Your name, address, and telephone number(s).

Curriculum vitae. The resume of a nuclear physicist.

Exit interview. The termination debriefing when you should say nice things about your former boss and everyone else.

Fired. Something you should avoid being. If it occurs, discuss a possible resignation with the firing authority.

Internal referral. Someone working for your potential employer who will act as your public relations representative.

Involuntary termination. One of two ways employment is severed. Generally refers to layoffs and termination for cause. The latter is the same as being fired, and requires the same corrective action.

Job comparability. The similarity between what you have done and what the employer is considering for you to do. Even if they appear totally different, 90 percent or more of every job is comparable. It's all in the eye of the beholder.

Job congruence. The extent to which the job being offered conforms to what you want to do. Your attitude should be that they are identical, or congruent.

Job description. An internal list of duties of a particular position. Looks good on paper, but tells you more about the individual who wrote it than the job.

Job order. Authorization to a placement service containing a summary of the position, salary range, and type of individual sought. Generally bears no similarity to the person eventually hired.

Job rotation. A system whereby some employers designate certain employees to rotate jobs, so each learns the functions of a certain activity.

Labor grade. A device used in wage and salary administration to rank jobs in order of their value and compensation.

New start ("new hire"). What you will be on your first day at Company X.

Offer. Something you receive as a result of packaging and selling yourself properly. [Often occurs at the time of the first interview after following the techniques in *Jeff Allen's Best: Get the Interview.*]

Opportunity. The employer has a great one for you.

Personal references. Those dependent on you for support or who owe you money.

Professional references. Former instructors, supervisors, coworkers, and other people familiar with your academic or occupational history and qualifications.

[See my book, *The Perfect Job Reference* (John Wiley & Sons, 1990) for a more complete definition of the two preceding terms and an effective guide for utilizing them.]

Qualifications. Combination of "quality," "fit," and "occupation." You have them.

Rate range. A device used in wage and salary administration to determine the lowest and highest amount that will be paid for a specific job. A critical consideration for incumbents in any position.

Resume. Something with your contact information, room for notes, job history, and enough class to generate an appointment for an interview. [See *Jeff Allen's Best: The Resume* for further instructions.]

Requisition ("rec"). The form that is initiated by a supervisor to obtain approval for hiring. Once the approval cycle is completed, it becomes an open requisition ("open rec").

Span of control. The number of subordinates a supervisor can handle effectively. Varies widely depending upon the capability of the supervisor, type of subordinates, complexity of the jobs, physical proximity, and amount of empire building permitted.

Voluntary termination. One of two ways employment is severed. Generally refers to leaving for a better position.[7]

Drop the dictionary on 'em!

52. Develop an action vocabulary.

The winners in life use certain words. If you use them, you too will sound like a winner. Then you'll feel like a winner. It will help you look like a winner.

Is it a "script"? Are you "acting"? If "being yourself" could get you hired, I'd recommend it. It won't, so it don't. Show me a job you got with no preparation, and I'll show you a job you were overqualified to do.

Dennis Waitley stated in *The Psychology of Winning*:

> Perhaps the most important key to the permanent enhancement of self-esteem is the practice of positive self talk. Every waking moment we must feed our subconscious self-images, positive thoughts about ourselves and our performances . . . so relentlessly and vividly that our self-images are in time modified to conform to the new, higher standards.

> Current research on the effect of words and images on the functions of the body offers amazing evidence of the power that words, spoken at random, can have on body functions monitored on bio-feedback equipment . . . that's why winners rarely "put themselves down" in actions or words.[8]

The following is a winner's word list:

Ability	Conceive
Accelerate	Concurrence
Accurate	Conduct
Active	Conscientious
Aggressive	Control
Agreement	Develop
Analyze	Diplomatic
Assertive	Direct
Attitude	Discipline
Capable	Drive
Careful	Dynamic
Common sense	Effective

Efficiency	Potential
Eliminate	Precise
Energetic	Pride
Enthusiastic	Produce
Establish	Professional
Evaluate	Proficiency
Excel	Provide
Excellence	Recommend
Expand	Reliable
Expedite	Responsible
Focus	Results
Generate	Simplify
Guide	Skill
Implement	Solve
Improve	Streamline
Incisive	Strengthen
Initiate	Success
Innovate	Synergy
Lead	Systematic
Listen	Tactful
Manage	Thorough
Monitor	Train
Motivate	Trim
Participate	Urgency
Perform	Vital
Persuade	Win

The list includes the most powerful words used by copywriters to sell goods and services. That's what you're doing, too. Selling yourself and your assistance to the highest bidder. Write copy that tells—and sells.

53. Write the winner's word list into your script.

Here's a technique for making winning words your words, and using them with ease: Write ten of the words from the list on your old business cards or some cut-up index cards. Place the cards in your wallet or purse. Take them out frequently during the early phase of your search and construct sentences about yourself. Use one word per sentence. Make it sound good.

After you've incorporated those ten words into your vocabulary, try ten more. Then another ten. Repeat until you have internalized this entire list. You—and others—will be amazed at the change in your speech and attitude. And at how quickly you get offers.

54. Choose and use success phrases.

Now that you know the winner's vocabulary, you can develop your own "success phrases." They score major points in interviews. Here are some of my favorites:

- Work is not only the way to make a living, it's the way to make a life.
- We become not what we think, but what we do.
- We must be self-made, or never made.
- As long as you stand in your own way, everything seems to be in your way.
- You never fail, you just give up.
- Procrastination is a roadblock in the path of success.
- When you try hard, you are almost there.
- The hardest work in life is resisting laziness.
- A glimpse of an opportunity is an opportunity wasted.
- The best investment you can make is in yourself.
- The people who succeed are the people who look for the opportunities they want; and if they don't find them, they make them.

Use these and others you like. Practice them until they sound natural, and you'll soon find your self-confidence naturally increasing.

Repeat them in front of your mirror in the morning. Rehearse them in your mind before each interview. Consciously say a few where appropriate, and watch the interviewer sit up and take notice. When it happens, you're psychologically being signed for the part.

55. Don't use trite phrases and tired cliches.

As I observed in *Finding the Right Job at Midlife*, this is often a midlifer's trap, but almost any jobseeker can fall into it. Be careful to avoid the following dusty, tired, condescending lines, as well as any sexist or discriminatory language.

"At my age . . ."

"Back in the days when . . ."

"Back then . . ."

"In the good old days . . ."

"It used to be that . . ."

"Listen, son . . ."

"Nowadays . . ."

"Old timers like me . . ."

". . . over the hill."

"The girls in the office."

". . . up in years."

"Way back when . . ."

"We used to . . ."

"When I was younger. . . "

"When I was your age . . ."

"When you get to be my age . . ."

"Years ago. . ."

Don't call the interviewer "honey" or "dear." Don't refer to grown women as "gals" or "girls" and men as "guys" or "boys." Don't bring out any prejudices or dislikes the interviewer may have.

56. Withhold your resume.

It has already served its purpose, unless you got to the interview without submitting one. If that's the case, come prepared with copies of your super-resume (perfected with the techniques discussed in *Jeff Allen's Best: The Resume*).

Plan to say success phrases that will help elaborate what's in it. If your resume has already been used, avoid referring to it. It's a direct-mail marketing device that gets interviews, not jobs.

57. Use the "tie-down" technique to move the interview along.

Listening and *questioning* properly is the way to win the interview and get the job. For the first few minutes of the interview, you're observing and determining how to proceed. You've been asked impossible questions and have delivered inspirational answers.

Now, you must ask questions—*carefully*. In the recruiter's rulebook, *Closing on Objections*, Paul Hawkinson wrote:

> Constant questioning can be grating, and if overused, can work against you. No one wants to feel that they are on the receiving end of the prosecutor's interrogatory and questions must be used sparingly to be really effective. But they are necessary because *selling is the art of asking the right questions* to get to the minor yes's that allow you to lead . . . to the major decision and major yes. The final placement is nothing more than the sum total of all your yes's throughout the process. Your job, then, is to nurse the process along. [Emphasis added][9]

Moving the process along is done through the use of "tie-down" phrases in questions designed to elicit an affirmative response. The most common ones are:

Aren't I/you/we/they?

Can't I/he/she/you/we/they/it?

Doesn't he/she/it?

Don't I/you/we/they?

Don't you agree?

Hasn't he/she/it?

Haven't I/you/we/they?

Isn't he/she/it?

Isn't that right?

Shouldn't I/he/she/you/we/they/it?

Wasn't I/he/she/it?

Weren't you/we/they?

Won't I/he/she/you/we/they/it?

Wouldn't I/he/she/you/we/they/it?

There are four kinds of "tie-downs," and you should vary your dialogue with them so you won't appear obvious or overbearing. With each agreement you obtain from the interviewer, you have scored one more "minor yes" leading up to that "major yes"—the offer.

58. The standard tie-down.

These are used at the end of the question:

"My qualifications appear to fit the position you have open, *don't they?*"

"Diversified Investments really has a lot to offer someone with my experience, *doesn't it?*"

"It looks like we'll be able to eliminate the problem, *don't you agree?*"

59. The inverted tie-down.

These are used at the beginning of a question:

"*Isn't it* an excellent position for someone with my background?"

"*Don't you* think we'll work together well?"

"*Wouldn't you* like to see how I can be of assistance?"

60. The internal tie-down.

These are used in the middle of a compound question:

"Since the entire data processing staff agrees, *shouldn't we* discuss when I can start work?"

"When the budget is approved, *won't it* expedite production to have someone who knows the project?"

"Now that we've had the opportunity to meet, *wouldn't it* be great to work together?"

61. The tag-on tie-down.

The final kind of tie-down is used after a statement of fact. A slight pause, then emphasis on the tie-down, improves its effect.

"My experience will benefit Allied Products, *won't it?*"

"You've really spent a lot of time and money to get the right person, *haven't you?*"

"This problem can be corrected easily, *can't it?*"

The best way to learn tie-down questioning techniques is the same way you rehearse your script for the interview. You write down all the tie-down lines you can use during the interview, then read them into a tape recorder and play them back once or twice a day—every day—to implant them into your subconscious. They'll pop out automatically when you need them.

After about a week of this exercise, the tie-down technique will come naturally to you. You can begin your dialogue with a general question, such as:

"National Manufacturing leads the market with this product, *doesn't it?*"

Then hone in for the win with questions such as:

"*Wouldn't it* be interesting to work for a supervisor like that?"

And, finally:

"*Shouldn't I* give notice?"

Remember: Overuse of questions will make you sound like you're auditioning for a game show rather than taking a screen test. Use them sparingly for best results.

---

62. Find an area of agreement, and lead slowly and carefully to the offer.

When you hear a positive comment, such as "This is the kind of experience we need," lean forward slightly in your seat, smile, and try one of these:

"My background fits this position very well."

"We have a good match here."

"This looks like a long-term situation."

"I'm excited about the position."

"Everything looks good."

These statements gently "close" the interviewer with class. He or she doesn't know and doesn't care whether you're using closing techniques. What matters is that you're a qualified candidate who knows how to perform on the set.

63. Be honest, not modest.

Over 65 percent of all candidates don't know how to handle a compliment. They're so ready to "overcome objections" that they're unprepared when a favorable response occurs.

When the interviewer says something like, "These are really impressive credentials," you should look pleased, smile, and say, "Thank you. It's been great developing my career. I'd like to continue doing so at Training Dimensions."

64. Say positive things about your present (or former) employer.

It may not be easy, but it's essential. A successful interview is a *positive* performance. Remember what I said about the words used by winners? They work.

If you are negative, you "negate" yourself. The interviewer perceives you as a malcontent who will do the same in your new job. You're associated with your present (or former) employer's success or failure, too. You were there, weren't you? If it succeeded, what did you contribute? If it failed, why didn't you make it succeed? Even if your former employer was a loser, accentuate the positive.

As Dr. Waitley noted in *The Psychology of Winning*:

> Winners focus on past successes and forget past failures. They use errors and mistakes as a way to learning—they dismiss them from their minds.
>
> . . . Winners know it doesn't matter how many times they

have failed in the past. What matters is their successes which should be remembered, reinforced, and dwelt upon.[10]

Access your action vocabulary, cite success phrases, and review your past in the best possible light.

---

65. Admire the achievements of the prospective employer.

However, do this only if the admiration is genuine, based on facts, and applied sparingly.

Use the information you acquired through your research and phonework to mention the employer's successes at appropriate places in the conversation. Your grasp of the situation will impress the interviewer.

Mention that the anticipated expansion will create new opportunities. Observe that multiple locations offer a chance to combine resources and streamline operations. Know *why* the company is a market leader for a certain product or process, and comment on it. Changes are *always* challenges—when you're a jobseeker.

---

66. Be observant.

Throughout the interview, look and listen to learn information that will help you. A successful interview requires the ability to think on your feet, move in your seat, and follow the beat. Undivided attention is necessary to seize opportunities as they arise.

Take out your pad with your gold pen, and take fast notes as you go—it makes you look professional. Write names, titles, buzzwords, products, and other items you can use in the follow-up stage. Don't reduce your eye contact with the interviewer, ask him or her to repeat anything, or ask how to spell something. If you do, you might as well write "O-U-T."

The pad and pen are professional props. Even if you never write anything down, you might not *need* any follow-up. Then that pad can be used for taking notes in your new-hire orientation.

67. Package a positive image.

Studies show that within an hour of your departure, 85 percent of your words will be forgotten. The only tangible things left from the encounter will be the documents you submitted and the interviewer's notes.

Leave a lasting impression in the 15 percent that's left. You want to pack these intangible items into an invisible package you'll leave with the interviewer:

- Enthusiasm
- Confidence
- Energy
- Dependability

These attributes are necessary for any job, and it doesn't take specific experience and skills to display them. If you are scoring direct hits with your image in these four areas, you'll be way out in front of all other candidates.

Then, there are four "subsidiary" attributes that also should be stressed. These show how you're an asset, not an expense:

- Loyalty
- Honesty
- Pride in work
- Service for value received

In professional, management, administrative, and clerical positions, add a final four:

- Efficiency

- Organization
- Economy
- Profit

INTERVIEW "DON'TS"

To keep your interviews irresistible, there are eight errors you absolutely should not make:

---

68. Don't smoke.

Asking for permission is just as bad as apologizing. Even if the interviewer consents, smoke is the last thing you want in the office. Smoking detracts from your perfectly prepared performance, interferes with your image, and leaves an offensive odor on breath, hair, hands, and clothes. That *isn't* the kind of lasting impression you want to leave.

Some companies have even banned smoking from their premises, or have permitted it only in limited areas. Even if the interviewer smokes, you shouldn't. Your chances of getting hired will go up in smoke.

This is no time to go through withdrawal, however. To avoid the jitters, try an over-the-counter nonsmoking tablet. Read the label, and choose one that has no warnings about blood pressure, heart conditions, or drowsiness. Those that mention these side effects generally contain either stimulants or sedatives that can affect your reactions. Use the tablets a few days before the interview so that you will be able to adjust to them and judge if there is any difference in your reactions.

---

69. Don't chew gum.

Farrah Rambo Einstein, Ph.D., wouldn't stand a chewing chance of getting hired.

70. Don't interrupt.

If you do so, you are out of sync. You're not leading or pacing. You're heading for the door. Bring yourself back into alignment, take control, and pace.

71. Don't object to discriminatory questions.

The interview is no place to take a stand. Don't even mention that a question is illegal. Just answer as pleasantly as possible. Being *right* may feel good, but being *nice* will win you the interview.

72. Don't look at your watch.

It's a bad signal. This and other indications that you are anxious, impatient, or not interested will pressure the interviewer and ruin the rapport you've been building.

   If you have another interview, or the 45-minute time limit is approaching, say, "This has been so interesting I can't believe 45 minutes have almost passed. I have another appointment, but can we get together again?" You never want to interview beyond 45 minutes with one person

73. Don't read any documents on the interviewer's desk.

Bad, bad manners—and annoying. Maintain eye contact with the interviewer.

74. Don't pick up any objects in the interviewer's office.

Many people closely identify with the objects in their office, particularly personal possessions. They may actually feel these things are extensions of themselves. Picking them up and handling them violates their air space and privacy. Even if nothing is said, resentment may cause the interviewer to terminate the interview early without comment.

75. Don't ask for the job.

Ignore advice to "ask for the job" as you would "ask for the sale." Everyone knows why you're there. Asking for the job lowers you. It's not a "sale." It's a "buy." *You're* a "buy."

76. Use the "magic four good-bye."

The way you say good-bye will etch your positive image into the interviewer's mind. Just as with your greeting, there are four steps to follow in precise order. They're the same as the "magic four hello," except for the third item:

1. A smile.
2. Direct eye contact.
3. The words, "It sounds like a great opportunity . . . I look forward to hearing from you."
4. A firm but gentle handshake.

An enticing exit will lead to a standing ovation. *Always* leave your audience wanting more.

Perfect for the Part!

You're off the stage, but they're still talking about your performance. The actors that followed you didn't even stand a chance. Now your interview follow-up will turn that talk into an offer.

Chapter

4

Getting the Part: Follow-up and Finishing Touches

Giving your all in the interview may leave you tired, but you're not hired—yet. You've got a way to go to get that offer. Your next steps are crucial ones. Before the cheer leaves your ear, shift into high gear.

A properly scripted, properly delivered interview performance, combined with diligent follow-up, produces the most offers. Correspondence, telephone calls, and networking keep you in front of the interviewer while you're out getting offers elsewhere.

But first you must be your own toughest critic, and . . .

77. Image the interview.

This step is a major reason for leaving time between interviews. You've got to get to a quiet place—even if it's only your car—and replay the interview in your head.

Try to see yourself and the interviewer interacting. Did you assess the interviewer's style accurately, align with him or her, pace, and lead? Did the interviewer smile and nod his or her head a lot? Did you sense positive reinforcement?

Go over the following checklist:

- Did I make a positive first impression with the "magic four hello"?
- Did the interviewer and I have rapport?
- Did I use tie-downs to secure agreement?

- Did I access my action vocabulary, winner's word list, and success phrases?
- Did I thank the interviewer?
- Did my closing statement lead into the next meeting?
- What did I do wrong?

78. Recap your revelations.

After mentally reviewing your performance, write down the facts. What did you learn about the job, the company? Note names of individuals, their titles, details about the organization, and anything else you can use for your follow-up letters and phone calls, second interviews, and negotiations.

79. Write your review.

As soon as possible after the interview, record all the facts about the company, the position available, and your interview performance on an "interview evaluation form." Your interviewer will be filling out his or her own. A sample you can use for yourself is on the next page.

80. Write a follow-up letter.

The follow-up letter is the single most effective post-interview technique you can use—if you use it right.

I'm not talking about a glorified thank-you note. A "better letter" takes what you learned in the interview and uses it to write sales copy that highlights your qualifications.

All those words you said during the interview have dwindled down to one or two remarks, and your image is fading fast. You have to keep from being confused with average applicants. A properly drafted letter will restate your candidacy.

Interview Evaluation

Interview day, date, and time: ———————————————

Name of company: ———————————————————

Address: ——————————————————————————

Phone: ———————————————————————————

Name of interviewer: ——————————————————

Title: ——————————————— Phone: ——————

Personal characteristics of interviewer: ——————

———————————————————————————————————

———————————————————————————————————

Title of position(s) available: ——————————————

Duties: ———————————————————————————

———————————————————————————————————

Reports to: (Name) ——————————— (Title) ————

Number of people supervised: —————————————

Salary range: —————————————————————————

Bonus or other benefits: ——————————————————

———————————————————————————————————

Salary review period: ——————————————————

Next career step: ————————————————————

Company information learned during interview: ————

———————————————————————————————————

My qualifications for position include: ———————

———————————————————————————————————

Any weaknesses I have relating to position: —————

———————————————————————————————————

Job assets: ———————————————————————————

Job liabilities: ——————————————————————

Review of my interview performance: ————————

———————————————————————————————————

Interviewer seemed most impressed by my: —————

———————————————————————————————————

My weakest areas during interview were: —————

———————————————————————————————————

———————————————————————————————————

———————————————————————————————————

(continued on next page)

Follow-up Plan:

Follow-up letters (name and date sent):

1. _____ Date: _____
2. _____ Date: _____
3. _____ Date: _____

Follow-up phone calls (name and date):

1. _____ Date: _____
2. _____ Date: _____
3. _____ Date: _____

Other follow-up (internal referrals and references):

1. _____ Date: _____
2. _____ Date: _____
3. _____ Date: _____

Plan of action and questions to ask in next interview: _____
_____
_____

81. Follow the better letter format.

I covered the subject of better letter format in the second book in this series, *Jeff Allen's Best: Get the Interview*. Just for review, the letter should:

- Be typed on high-quality personal letterhead, on an electronic typewriter with a carbon ribbon or on a word processor with a letter-quality printer, in block format. No errors or erasures.

- Be no longer than one page.

- Be fully addressed with no abbreviations, misspellings, or inaccuracies.

- Contain the middle initial and title of the interviewer. (Double check exact title and spellings.)

- Be brief, enthusiastic, and to the point.

82. Create the content carefully.

You only have a small amount of space, so use it to your best advantage. Accentuate your assets and accomplishments, and convincingly describe how you can benefit the employer. Include the properly spelled names of people you met and buzzwords familiar to the interviewer. End with words similar to the magic four good-bye, requesting a reply as soon as possible.

Here is a sample from *How to Turn an Interview into a Job.* You can adapt the letter to the target job and personality of the interviewer.

1. ADDRESS LINE

    The full company name, full address (no abbreviations), full name of the interviewer, and his or her full title. These make you look thorough and professional.

2. SUBJECT LINE

    "Re: Interview for the Position of *(title)* on *(date)."*

    This zeroes in on the contents and dresses up the letter.

3. GREETING

    "Dear Mr./Ms. *(last name):"*

    "Miss or "Mrs." should not be used unless you know the interviewer does so. First names are out of the question even if they were used during the interview.

4. OPENING

    a. "It was a pleasure meeting with you last (day) to discuss the opening in *(department)* with Company X."

    b. "I appreciated meeting with *(name)* and yourself in your office on *(day)* to discuss the *(title)* position with Company X."

    c. Thanks again for taking the time to see me regarding the opening in *(department).*

    Again, comment on or add to something discussed during your interview in the body of the letter. Choose a topic that allows you to emphasize directly or implicitly your qualifications. This will keep your follow-up from being just another routine thank-you.

5. BODY

    a. "From our discussion, and the fine reputation of your organization, it appears that the *(title)* position would enable me to fully use my background in
        _____."

    b. "I was particularly impressed with the professionalism evident throughout my visit. Company X appears to have the kind of environment I have been seeking."

    c. "The atmosphere at Company X seems to strongly favor individual involvement, and I would undoubtedly be able to contribute significantly to its goals."

6. CLOSING

    a. "While I have been considering other situations, I have deferred a decision until I hear from you. Therefore, your prompt reply would be greatly appreciated."

    b. "It's an exciting opportunity, and I look forward to hearing your decision very soon."

    c. "The *(title)* position and Company X are exactly what I have been seeking, and I hope to hear from you within the next week."

7. SALUTATION

    "Sincerely,"

    "Very truly yours,"

    "Best regards,"[11]

83. Don't fiddle around.

Get that letter in the mail *now*. It should arrive no later than three days after your interview. If you interviewed on a Monday or Tuesday, have it there by Wednesday or Thursday. Since Fridays and Mondays are overload times, letters that follow Wednesday or Thursday interviews can be timed for arrival the following Tuesday.

Fast follow-up avoids the effect of the "fiddle theory." It was developed by Robert Ringer in his bestseller, *Winning Through Intimidation*:

> The longer a person fiddles around with something, the greater the odds that the result will be negative. . . . In the case of Nero, Rome burned; in the case of a sale, the longer it takes to get to a point of closing, the greater the odds that it will never close.

> As a general rule, you should assume that time is always against you when you try to make a deal—any kind of deal. There's an old saying about "striking while the iron's hot," and my experience has taught me that it certainly is a profound statement in that circumstances always seem to have a way of changing.[12]

84. Take a deep breath—and call the interviewer.

In the second book of this series, *Jeff Allen's Best: Get the Interview*, I discussed the deep breath phone call, quoting Michael Korda from *Power! How to Get It, How to Use It*:

> "The person who receives a telephone call is always in an inferior position of power to the person who placed it."[13]

Knowing that, if you haven't received a response to your follow-up letter within a week, pick up the phone, take a deep breath, *smile*, and call the interviewer. If you've been interviewed by a department supervisor or other decision maker rather than a personneler, the technique is a little different. I discussed the approach to use in *How to Turn an Interview into a Job*:

> . . . [E]nlist the executive's secretary or assistant as your ally, not your adversary. A courteous, firm tone of voice works wonders. Don't play guessing games to get around the front desk: an executive calling an executive always states his name. Only nobodies have no names. And don't ask nosy

questions about the boss's schedule, hoping to catch him unguarded. A good secretary simply will not tell you. In any case, if you call very early (before 9:00 a.m.) or late (after 5:00 p.m.) you can often get [through] directly.

If you speak to the secretary:

Secretary: Good morning. Mr. (last name)'s office.

You: This is *(first name) (last name)* calling. May I speak to him, please?

Secretary: I'm sorry, he's stepped away from his desk/on another line/in a meeting. May I take a message?

You: Mr. *(last name)* and I met last week regarding the *(title)* position.

Secretary: One minute, please.

The boss might very well have stepped away from his desk, be on another line, or in a meeting. But more than likely the secretary is checking to see if he wants to take the call or not. If not:

You: When would be a good time to call back? *or* I'll hold, please.

Since you have been direct and helpful, the secretary is very likely to return the courtesy. Also be polite and stubborn: you'll get the decision maker and a decision before long.[14]

It's your livelihood on the line. So don't let anyone keep you hanging.

85. Call your references.

In *The Perfect Job Reference*, I taught jobseekers how to use targeted reference cover letters to get an interview. It pointed out that once you've been through an interview, the interviewer will probably be calling your references to verify your credentials and ask for more information.

Beat the interviewer to the punch. Call the references whose names you've given, and fill them in on how the interview went. Tell them about the job, and how your qualifications fit it. Doing so will get them an Academy Award nomination for "best performance by a reference in a supporting role" from the Applicant Academy.

86. Recontact your internal referrals.

Check in by phone with any internal referrals and friends you made during your research of the target employer. Tell them a few positive things about the interview. Inquire subtly if they've "heard anything." If they're receptive, ask them to "put in a good word" for you.

87. Prepare for your encore performance.

If you've followed the first ten techniques in this section, you'll be called back for a second interview. And the second interview is *almost* equated with getting the job.

Statistically, this is true 60 percent of the time. However, there are crucial differences from your first visit. If you understand them and use them to your advantage, you can almost guarantee that you *will* be hired. Here's how to do it once more with feeling, from *How to Turn an Interview into a Job*:

> If your first interview was in the personnel department, you will often be asked to return for another meeting. This will probably be with the supervisor and others in the department that has the job opening, which personnel calls the functional department.

> If you already made direct contact with the supervisor, and your second interview is with the personnel department, then you've probably already won the battle. That second interview then is merely a formality. Watching someone use a rubber stamp doesn't require much training.

"[S]upervisor" means any functional hiring authority from the chief executive officer down.

The differences are subtle. . . . Generally, you have passed through the interviewer's office and will be working on your future supervisor. This means that you *must* use every means at your disposal to understand what makes him tick.

At this point, you should have several acquaintances within the company that you can contact. If you haven't developed them, now is the time.

One ally you probably have overlooked is the interviewer himself. He has stamped you with his seal of approval, and you can help him by closing the requisition. The interviewer also knows that if he allows too many applicants to become actual candidates, the supervisor will delay making a decision. With so many seemingly qualified people, the supervisor's decision is that much more difficult.

Call the interviewer, and after expressing your appreciation, lead into the discussion with a comment something like: "From what I understand, it looks like I'll really be able to assist _____. Is there anything I should know before we meet?"

Then listen and take notes. The interviewer will be delighted to give you his impressions. Often they are extremely incisive since he has access to the personnel files. Before you conclude the conversation, ask the interviewer if he thinks the supervisor would mind a direct call. Interpret his "No, I don't." as a suggestion that you do so.

Then call the supervisor. After saying that the interviewer suggested you call him and asking if he has a few minutes, state: "I'm looking forward to meeting you (again) on _____, at _____. Before we get together, I wonder if there's anything you'd like me to bring."

The supervisor will not be able to think that fast. In the remote event he asks for something, evaluate whether it can affect your chances adversely. If so, say something like: "I'll check to see if I have it. If not, I'll bring what I can."

This is more than just an excuse to confirm the interview. It is a chance to hear where the supervisor's thinking is going to be with regard to hiring you. A little industrial espionage goes a long way. And you don't have far to go.[15]

Generally, the second interview is more *directed*. It takes one of two paths, and you should prepare for both. The first is:

88. The "Who Are You?" interview.

This is similar to the first interview, with the interviewer asking you a lot of questions and you delivering perfectly timed responses. The difference is that you've now developed a clearer profile of your interviewer and the target job (with a little help from your friends) and know what drives the audience wild. Then there's . . .

89. The "What Can You Do for Us?" interview.

This interview tends to be informational rather than personal. Review your scripts and your notes to rehearse the buzzwords, inside information, and technical data. Be prepared to demonstrate exactly how your background, experience, and skills enable you to do the target job. It's a more objective approach, and you can be fully prepared.

90. Negotiate the terms of employment.

Even before the second interview is over, you'll know if an offer is on its way. Phrases like, "when you start" and "your role would be . . ." tell you they already imagine you in the position.

This is an excellent time to customize the position to your needs as well as the employer's.

If accepting their offer would require relocation, learn exactly how much leeway you have in a starting date. You don't want to start a new position under the pressure of a rushed move, an unsold house, and a frantic family. Inquire about the company's relocation assistance.

91. Clarify the job description.

Analyze the positions below and above the target job. If the title is "manager" but there is no one reporting to you, determine just how much authority and support you will have.

If the position is new, find out how yours will relate to other positions in the company. Some creative negotiating now will make the target job much easier.

92. Secure a star's salary.

Negotiating a salary is much like negotiating a loan: The more you look like you need it, the less likely you are to get it.

If a salary or "range" is mentioned in your first or second interviews, don't react. If you directly are asked to disclose your current salary, give an amount that reflects the value of anticipated raises, upcoming bonuses, overtime, pay in lieu of vacation, and so on.

Your new salary should be a 10 to 20 percent increase over your current (or last) salary. If relocation is involved, 20 percent is the minimum. If the new position involves an increase in responsibility, that should be reflected.

Know all of this going into your salary negotiations, and write down your justification. You'll get justice (unlike after you become an employee).

93.   Get an offer in writing.

Once a verbal offer has been made, request a written offer by mail within a week. If you don't, write your own follow-up letter outlining the terms. Send it, and follow up immediately with the hiring authority to make sure you both agree.

94.   Evaluate the offer.

Now that you've interviewed, second interviewed, negotiated, and secured an offer, it's time to decide if it's *the* offer. With your interviewing skills, it's not the only one you'll get.

Evaluating a job offer requires you to consider carefully some important factors. They include the usual—salary, benefits, and career potential—as well as others you might not have considered.

What will the working environment be like? How will it differ from what you are used to? If relocation is involved, how will your family be effected? Peak performance on the new job will be aided by a supportive, organized personal life.

If you're out of work now, you may not feel you have the luxury of choosing. But you do. You owe it to yourself, your family, and your employer to find the best possible job from an infinite inventory.

95.   Accept with assurance.

After evaluating the new job and deciding that it's a good opportunity, demonstrate confidence in your decision. The way you accept will set the stage for future negotiations after you start work. If you writhe in pain, then make a qualified acceptance ("Okay, I'll take it, but . . ."), you'll start off on the wrong foot. It will be stuck on a floodlight. Things can heat up rather quickly like that.

Make sure the offer is right, then go for it. Shake hands, smile, and emphasize how much you're "looking forward" to the "new challenge." In fact, you're "anticipating" the "opportunity" to "contribute."

96. Resign with refinement.

Don't burn any bridges. It takes forever to rebuild them, even if you don't get lost looking. Give proper notice, help in the hiring of your replacement, and train him or her if you can.

97. Leave 'em laughing.

You never know when you'll meet up with these coworkers and supervisors again. You may need them. Remember your networking lessons. Keep in touch.

98. Get a reference letter.

As I noted in *The Perfect Job Reference*:

> The time to get a reference letter from a supervisor is before your coworkers cut your cake. . . . This letter will come in handy in the future if your supervisor runs away from home, goes crazy, dies, or tries to block your career path.[16]

Before you ask for a reference letter, review your accomplishments and results in the position you are leaving, and draft a sample letter. Chances are your supervisor will sign with a sigh (of relief—because he or she won't have to prepare one).

99. Thank your supporting cast.

Don't forget to "take care of your people"—those outside and inside the new employer who assisted. A phone call, a sincere letter, or a thoughtful gift will let them know you appreciated the help—and keep your "net working" for you.

---

100. Begin again.

It's your first day on the new job. But some day—hopefully not too soon—you're going to want to move up, on, or out.

Write down your accomplishments in your new job so that when it comes time to write a resume, you'll be ready. Keep your contacts continuing and your options open. While your job is a priority, your *career* is even more important. Give it at least equal time.

I wrote *Surviving Corporate Downsizing* to help conscientious employees take charge of their careers. If you don't want to be at the mercy of others, get a copy and follow its advice.

There's no feeling in the world like being able to get yourself hired any place, any time, on your own terms.

"Best" wishes for success!

Conclusion

Now you know why this third book in the series is entitled *Jeff Allen's Best: Win the Job*. Because auditioning successfully—getting hired—is a game. Using the 100 techniques, you'll play to win.

Oh, there will always be other advice out there for jobseekers. But there is a big difference between *advising* and *assisting*. For you, it's the difference between *getting tired* and *getting hired*.

And once you can get hired—any place, any time—you'll know the true meaning of security, freedom, and self-fulfillment.

All the best for a lifetime of success!

Endnotes

1. Molloy, John T., *John T. Molloy's New Dress for Success.* New York: Warner Books, 1988.

2. Allen, Jeffrey G., J.D., C.P.C., *The Complete Q&A Job Interview Book.* New York: John Wiley & Sons, 1989.

3. Allen, Jeffrey G., J.D., C.P.C., and Jess Gorkin, *Finding the Right Job at Midlife.* New York: Simon & Schuster, 1985.

4. Zunin, Leonard, M.D., with Natalie Zunin, *Contact: The First Four Minutes.* New York: Ballantine Books, 1973.

5. Korda, Michael, *Power! How to Get It, How to Use It.* New York: Ballantine Books, 1975.

6. Allen, Jeffrey G., J.D. C.P.C., *How to Turn an Interview into a Job.* New York: Simon & Schuster, 1981, pp. 40–41.

7. *Ibid*, pp. 41–43.

8. Waitley, Dennis E., Ph.D., *The Psychology of Winning.* Chicago: Nightingale-Conant, 1979.

9. Hawkinson, Paul A., *Closing on Objections.* St. Louis, MO: The Kimberly Organization, 1983.

10. Waitley.

11. Allen, *How to Turn an Interview Into a Job*, pp. 79–80.

12. Ringer, Robert J., *Winning Through Intimidation.* New York: Fawcett Crest Books, 1973.

13. Korda.

14. Allen, *How to Turn an Interview into a Job*, p. 81.

15. Ibid., pp. 66–67.

16. Allen, Jeffrey G., J.D., C.P.C., *The Perfect Job Reference*. New York: John Wiley & Sons, 1990, p. 95.

Bibliography

Allen, Jeffrey G., J.D., C.P.C., *The Complete Q&A Job Interview Book*. New York: John Wiley & Sons, 1989.

Allen, Jeffrey G., J.D., C.P.C., and Jess Gorkin, *Finding the Right Job at Midlife*. New York: Simon & Schuster, 1985.

Allen, Jeffrey G., J.D. C.P.C., *How to Turn an Interview into a Job*. New York: Simon & Schuster, 1981.

Allen, Jeffrey G., J.D., C.P.C., *Jeff Allen's Best: Get the Interview*. New York: John Wiley & Sons, 1990.

Allen, Jeffrey G., J.D., C.P.C., *Jeff Allen's Best: The Resume*. New York: John Wiley & Sons, 1990.

Allen, Jeffrey G., J.D., C.P.C., *The Perfect Job Reference*. New York: John Wiley & Sons, 1990.

Allen, Jeffrey G., J.D., C.P.C., *Surviving Corporate Downsizing*. New York: John Wiley & Sons, 1988.

Fast, Julius, *Body Language*. New York: Pocket Books, 1982.

Hawkinson, Paul A., *Closing on Objections*. The Kimberly Organization: P.O. Box 31011, St. Louis, MO, 63131, 1983 ($25—Must be ordered directly from the publisher).

Korda, Michael, *Power! How to Get It, How to Use It*. New York: Ballantine Books, 1975.

Molloy, John T., *John T. Molloy's New Dress for Success*. New York: Warner Books, 1988.

Waitley, Dennis E., Ph.D., *The Psychology of Winning*. Chicago: Nightingale-Conant, 1979.

Index

Acceptance, 95, 127–128
Action words, 98–100
Actor factor, 3–4, 28
Applications, 14
Attache case, 17–18
Attitude, 33, 87–88, 106, 108

Behavior modification, 13
Body Language, 30
Body language, 30
Buzzwords, 21, 50, 81, 95–97

Caffeine, 18
Career objective questions
    changing goals, 58–59
    importance of goals, 56–57
    long-term goals, 58, 60
    promotions, 60
    relocation, 59
    short-range goals, 58
    tenure with company, 57–58
    wanting a particular job, 57
Character questions
    aptitudes, 42–43
    attendance, 43
    competitiveness, 45
    intelligence, 40–41
    job security, 41
    people skills, 43, 44
    quirks, 44
    reading material, 44–45
    reasons for success, 41–42

teamwork, 43
values, 44
Checklist, follow-up, 115–116
Child care, 33
Closing on Objections, 102
Closing techniques, 106–107
College degree, 35
Commuting distance, 32
Complete Q&A Job Interview Book, The, 23, 27
Consistency, 10
Contact information, 95
Contact: The First Four Minutes, 30, 87
Corporate culture, 12
Curriculum vitae, 95

Deep breath phone call, 121–122
Dress (*see* Fashion)

Education
    background, 34–36
    choice of major, 36–37
    continuing, 38
    family influence on, 36
    future goals for, 38
    grades, 39–40
    as preparation for job, 37–38, 39
    records, 35
Exit interview, 95

Experience and training questions
  career start, 72–73
  employment history, 75
  quality of work, 73–74
  and reason for leaving current position, 73
  strengths, 74–75
  success factors, 74
  supervisors' evaluations, 76
Eye contact, 22, 86, 107, 110, 111

Family questions (see Personal Questions)
Family/work balance, 33
Fashion
  exceptions to rules, 18
  men, 15–16
  outerwear, 22
  sunglasses, 22
  women, 16–17
Fast, Julius, 30
Feedback, 81
Finding the Right Job at Midlife, 35
Firing (see Termination)
First impressions, 14, 85–86
Follow-up
  imaging, 115–117
  letter, 116–117, 118–121
  plan, 118
  and recapping, 116–117
  telephone call, 121–122
Form of address, 87

Gum chewing, 109

Halo effect, 93
Handshake, 86–87
Hawkinson, Paul, 102
Health, 34

Home ownership, 32
How to Turn an Interview into a Job, 4, 93, 95, 119, 123
Hygiene, 17, 19

Image (see Fashion)
Imaging, 115–116
Initiative and creativity questions
  attitude, 46–47
  decision making, 49–50
  job effectiveness, 46
  pressure, 47
  problem solving, 46
  role models, 48–49
  success measurement, 47–48
  supervision, 49
Internal referrals, 96, 123
Interview-to-offer ratio, 4–5
Interviewer
  aligning with, 92–94
  assessment of, 88
  feedback, 81
  form of address for, 87
  pacing, 81
  personality types, 88–92
  and using buzzwords, 81
Interviews
  career objective questions, 56–60
  character questions, 40–45
  and current employer, 106–107
  don'ts, 109–111
  education questions, 34–40
  experience and training questions, 72–76
  first impressions, 14
  initiative and creativity questions, 45–50
  and leverage, 14

management ability ques-
tions, 50–56
and meals, 10–11, 20
opening greeting for, 86
outside interests questions,
76–80
overstatement during, 31
personal questions, 30–34
and questioning the interviewer, 80–82
salary questions, 68–72
second, 11, 19–20, 123–126
talking by interviewee in, 81
target job questions, 60–68
techniques for , 85–112
timing of, 10, 20–22
while employed, 65
Involuntary termination, 96

*Jeff Allen's Best: Get the
Interview,* 9, 11, 96, 121
Jeff Allen's Best: The Resume,
56, 95, 102
Job comparability, 96
Job congruence, 96
Job description, 96, 126
Job order, 96
Job requisition, 28
Job rotation, 96
*John T. Molloy's New Dress for
Success,* 15

Knockout factors, 30
Korda, Michael, 92

Labor grade, 96
Labor pool, 95
Language
ability, 33
insider, 95–97
Likability, 93

Magic four
goodbye, 111
hello, 86
Makeup (*see* Fashion)
Management ability questions
communication skills, 53
decision making, 54
delegating responsibility, 55
financial responsibility, 55–56
hiring, 52
management abilities, general,
51–53
staff relations, 50–51, 54, 56
terminating employees, 53–54
Military service, 31, 71
Modesty, 106
Molloy, John T., 15

National Placement Law Center,
4
Negotiation
salary, 126
terms of employment,
125–126
Networking, 128
New start, 96
Note-taking, 107–108

Offer, 96, 127
Opportunity, 97
Outside income, 71
Outside interests
alcohol use, 79
extracurricular activities in
high school, 78
leadership, 79
leisure, 77
matching with company,
76–77
self-improvement, 80
social life, 79–80

Outside interests (*continued*)
  sports, 77
  television viewing, 78–79
Overstatement, 31

Pacing
  avoiding cliches, trite phrases,
    101–102
  definition of, 93–94
  and interrupting, 110
  and language use, 95–97
  and mirroring, 94–95
  and seating arrangement, 94
Perfect Job Reference, The, 122,
  128
Personal questions, 30–34
Personal references, 97
Personnel office, exit interviews,
  10
Placement law, 4
Post-interview techniques (*see*
  Follow-up)
*Power! How to Get It, How to
  Use It*, 92, 121
Professional references, 97
Programmed interviewing (*see*
  Script)
Psychology of Winning, 98
Punctuality, 20–22

Qualifications, 97
Questioning, interviewee,
  103–104

Rate range, 97
*Reader's Guide to Periodical
  Literature, The*, 12
References, 67, 122–123, 128–129
Referrals, internal, 14
Rehearsing, and taping, 29–30
Rejection, 5

Requisition ("rec"), 97
Research, 60, 61
  phone, 13
  of prospective employer,
    11–12, 107
  sources, 11
Residence, 31
Resignation, 128
Resume, 97, 102
Ringer, Robert, 121
Roles, 87–88

Salary
  base plus perks, 72
  constraints, 68–69
  current figure, 72
  employee's worth, 69
  future, 70
  history, 70–71
  lowering expectations, 71
  negotiation, 126
  outside income, 71
  as reward, 69–70
Scheduling (*see* Timing)
Script, 23, 29 (*see also* Interviews)
Smoking, 109
Span of control, 97
Spouse employment, 33
Stereotyping, 85
Surviving Corporate Downsizing, 129

Taping, 29–30
Target job questions
  availability, 61
  benefit to company, 64–65
  contacting previous employer,
    67
  edge over other candidates, 66
  industry trends, 63

interest in company, 63–64
interviewing while employed,
    65–66
knowledge of company, 61–62
knowledge of competitors,
    62–63
knowledge of position, 62
overqualifications, 67–68
overtime, 61
readiness for advance, 66
special qualifications, 65
suitability, 60
Telephobia, 13
Termination, 95
Tie-down technique
    internal, 104
    inverted, 104

standard, 103
tag-on, 104–105
Timing
    consistency, 10
    of follow-up letter, 120–121
    the interview, 9

Vocabulary, 95–97, 98–100
Voluntary termination, 97

Waitley, Dennis, 98
Winning Through Intimidation,
    121
*Woman's Dress for Success
    Book,The*, 15

Zunin, Leonard, 30, 87